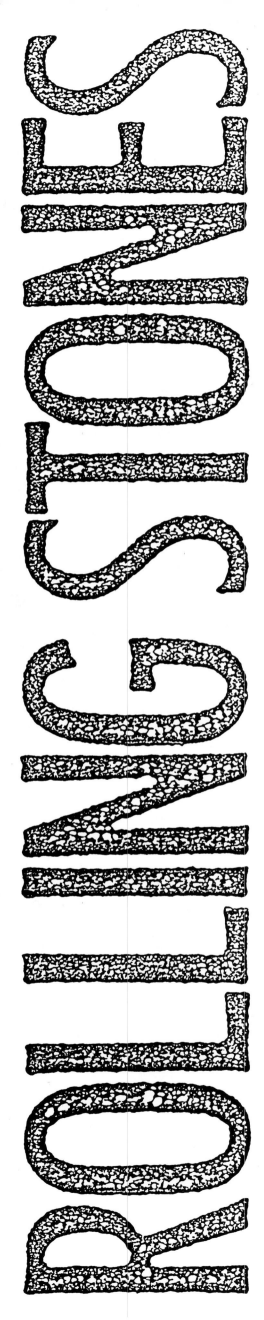

# THE ROLLING STONES

# A PICTORIAL HISTORY

# ROLLING STONES

# THE ROLLING STONES

# A PICTORIAL HISTORY

.

# MARIE CAHILL

# CONTENTS

Published by Grange Books
An imprint of Books & Toys Ltd
The Grange
Grange Yard
London SE1 3AG

Produced by
Bison Books Ltd
Kimbolton House
117A Fulham Road
London SW3 6RL

ISBN 1-85627-035-1

Printed in Hong Kong

Page 1: The Rolling Stones—the World's Greatest Rock and Roll band—in 1989...and (page 2-3) much earlier in their careers, before the death of Brian Jones. Page 5: In 1981, the Stones played to sold-out stadiums across the United States.

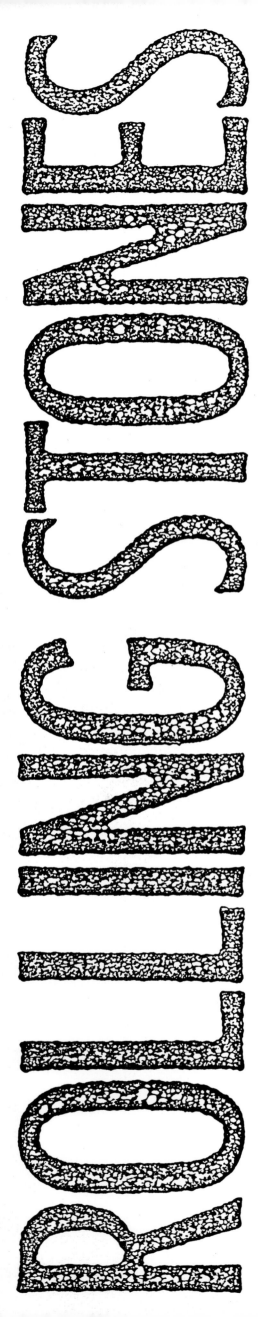
ROLLING STONES

# THE EARLY DAYS

I t was the spring of 1960. Mick Jagger, clutching the albums of Chuck Berry, Little Walter and Muddy Waters under his arm, was on his way to the London School of Economics, when he ran into Keith Richards*, a classmate from his grammar school days. Each was surprised to find that the other had similar taste in music—a passion for rhythm and blues.

Mick Jagger and Dick Taylor, another grammar school friend, had a band called Little Boy Blue and the Blue Boys. Since Richards shared their enthusiasm for American black urban blues, they invited him to join their band. Unlike the others, however, Keith saw the band as something more than just playing music for their own enjoyment. He envisioned the band earning money playing in clubs on weekends—nothing that would make them rich, of course, just enough to give them some spending money. And so it came to pass—the genesis of the Rolling Stones, the greatest rock and roll band in the world.

Michael Philip Jagger was born on 26 July 1943 in Dartford, England, the son of Eva and Joe Jagger. Contrary to his later image as a rebellious Rolling Stone, as a child he was a conventional, average boy, but even as a youngster he was known for his talent at mimicry and his boundless energy.

Keith Richards was also born in Dartford, on 18 December 1943, a few months after Jagger. Unlike Jagger, however, he was a true

*Early in his career, Keith dropped the 's' off of Richards and went by the name Keith Richard. The 's' was later (circa 1977-1978) returned to its rightful spot.

hooligan, an image that bore him ill fruit in his youth and nearly killed him as an adult, but which helped to create the essence of the band that would make him rich. Keith was expelled from Dartford Technical School for truancy when he was a teenager. Always the rebel, his later run-ins with authority would have far more serious ramifications. Keith eventually ended up in Sidcup Art School, only to drop out later on. Art school is where bright students who were discipline problems were sent, and in that era, there were more guitarists, such as John Lennon, 'studying art' than there were artists.

About the time Keith Richards and Mick Jagger were becoming reacquainted, Brian Jones was playing with Blues Incorporated, a blues band with a jazz influence. Brian Jones was born Lewis Brian Hopkins-Jones in Cheltenham on 28 February 1942. As a child, Brian was a quiet, well-behaved and well-liked boy, but as he entered his teens he grew increasingly rebellious. One of those rare gifted individuals, Brian had a talent for almost any musical instrument. His mother was a piano teacher, but by the time Brian was ten he was so proficient that he was beyond her skills. When he discovered the clarinet and then the saxophone, he quickly learned how to play each one. The music of Charlie Parker turned him on to

American jazz, and as Brian became more and more fanatical about playing jazz, his school work deteriorated.

Weekends were spent with a jazz band that played small clubs in the West Country. He earned a few shillings a night, but soon tired of the music as well as his job at an architect's office. Faced with the responsibility of becoming a father at fifteen, he took off for Scandinavia with his saxophone and the guitar he was learning to play. When he returned, now proficient on the guitar, he continued to play in jazz bands, but with a growing frustration because the jazz wasn't real jazz to him, but rather an English pop version, so Brian turned to Elmore James and the blues and eventually wound up in Blues Incorporated. The first time Jagger and Richards heard Brian Jones play the bottleneck guitar they were so enthralled by his performance they literally dragged him off the stage. Jagger and Richards immediately recognized that Brian's musical talents and knowledge exceeded their own.

Soon after that first meeting, Brian and Keith began jamming together, with Keith sometimes joining the jazz band that Brian played in. Keith's music had too much of a rock edge to it to suit the jazz purists, and Brian concluded that the best course of action would be to form a band of their own so that they could play their kind of music. And so the Rolling Stones were born.

*Left and page 7: The Rolling Stones pose for an early publicity shot aboard the HMS Discovery in 1963, the year their first single—'Come On'—was released. It's hard to believe that these innocent looking lads would soon be labeled the bad boys of rock and roll.*

*In contrast to the cute antics on the HMS Discovery, the photo on the far left provides a more realistic look at Mick Jagger, Charlie Watts, Bill Wyman, Brian Jones, and Keith Richards. The man between Watts and Wyman is Liverpool photographer Sam Lipson.*

Named after the Muddy Waters song 'Rollin' Stone,' the Rolling Stones of July 1962 consisted of Brian Jones; Keith Richards; Mick Jagger; Dick Taylor on bass; Ian Stewart, a Jones recruit who played boogie woogie piano; and Tony Chapman on drums. Dick Taylor soon left the band to continue his art schooling, and the Stones replaced him with Bill Wyman.

Born William Perks on 24 October 1936, Wyman (he changed his name after his stint in the Royal Air Force) was working for an engineering firm and playing part-time with a band called the Cliftons when he first met the Stones. With a wife and a year-old son to support, he was worried about making ends meet if he joined the Rolling Stones. An accomplished musician, Wyman played the organ, clarinet and piano as well as guitar and bass. In addition to his musical abilities, the Stones were equally impressed with his other assets—a speaker and two amplifiers.

Tony Chapman, a salesman whose job kept him on the road instead of in the band, was eventually replaced by Charlie Watts. When he was about 14, Charlie, who was born in London on 2 June 1941, took the neck off his banjo and turned it into a drum. Fortunately, his parents had the foresight to buy him a drum kit. It took several months for the Rolling Stones to coax Watts, who was the drummer for Blues Incorporated, to quit his full-time job at an advertising agency. The future as a drummer in a start-up band did not promise the security that his then current occupation did.

At first, jobs for the Rolling Stones were scarce and sometimes didn't pay, but the band was generally optimistic. To earn a bit of cash, they would collect empty beer bottles and return them to pubs. Jagger was still attending the London School of Economics. Intelligent—but hardly into his studies—Jagger wasn't quite prepared to forsake a traditional career in business for the life of a musician.

By February 1963, the club dates were fairly steady, with the Stones usually playing four nights a week. They were making progress and Jagger and Richards began to think that the band was about to make it big. Giorgio Gomelsky, a local entrepreneur, booked the Stones for his dance club—the Crawdaddy—in Richmond, a town about 40 miles south of Soho. Every Sunday, for eight months, the Crawdaddy Club was the place to be. The young, the hip and the campy descended on the Crawdaddy Club, fascinated by Jagger's sex appeal and by the band's vibrant sound.

Giorgio, who took a paternal interest in the boys, became the Stones' unofficial manager. He dreamed of the Rolling Stones becoming as big as the Beatles. In 1963, the Beatles took London and then the world by storm. It was the year of Beatlemania. Not only were their records the hottest thing around, but fans clad in collarless 'Beatle jackets' began sporting 'Beatle haircuts.' Maybe, just maybe, the Stones would become famous too.

One of Giorgio's first promotional efforts for the Rolling Stones was to contact Peter Jones, a freelance writer specializing in pop music. Jones was so impressed by what he saw *and* heard that he went straight to the offices of the *Record Mirror* and talked journalist Norman Jopling into going down to Richmond to write a feature article on the Stones. Jopling's article, which was the first on the Stones to appear in a trade paper, had nothing but praise for the Rolling Stones, declaring that they were destined to be the biggest group in the R & B scene.

About the time the *Record Mirror* article appeared, Andrew Loog Oldham, a hustler on the edge of the new pop scene, became the Rolling Stones' official manager. Oldham's previous credits included a brief stint as the Beatles' manager, and he was recognized throughout the music industry as someone who knew what was hot. Cultivating the seeds of the Stones' bad boy image, Oldham—with financial backing from Eric Easton—promoted the

**These pages:** *Under the guidance of manager Andrew Loog Oldham, the Rolling Stones began appearing on British television and in clubs around London. Oldham's first major coup was an appearance on* **Thank Your Lucky Stars,** *timed to coincide with the release of 'Come On.' For a time, Oldham made them dress in jackets or leather vests, but eventually Jagger won the clothing wars.*

group as a nasty alternative to the Beatles. Oldham eased out Ian Stewart, claiming Stu was too clean cut to fit the bad boy image and that six was too many faces in a picture to remember. Stu, however, would not be eased out completely, staying on as a studio musician for many of their later recordings. He would remain a Stone at heart until his death in 1985.

## 'COME ON'

Oldham and Easton's first task was to buy back the tapes of five songs the Stones had recorded at IBC Studios in January and February of 1963. They then formed their own company—Impact Sound—to supervise the Stones' recording sessions and signed the band with Decca.

The Rolling Stones released their first single, Chuck Berry's 'Come On' backed with 'I Want To Be Loved' on 7 June 1963. (It would be ten years before that single was released in the United States.) Given their lack of expertise, it's amazing that the single was even released. Neither Oldham nor the Stones knew anything about making a record, so Oldham left the mixing of that all-important first single to studio engineer Roger Savage. Predictably, the results had the executives at Decca shaking their heads in dismay. The tape was so bad the Stones were asked to record it again at Decca's West Hampstead studios.

The same day their single was released, the Stones made their first television appearance on *Thank Your Lucky Stars,* a pop music show. Against Jagger's wishes, Oldham and Easton made the group dress in suits, insisting that was the only way they would be allowed on the BBC, thus opening the door to more exposure. Oldham was treading a fine line. He wanted the band to be perceived as rough and raunchy, but 'clean' enough for the BBC's standards. He got what he wanted: viewers wrote in complaining about the band's disgraceful appearance, particularly Jagger's long hair and blatant sexuality. Recognizing that controversy breeds recognition, Oldham was delighted with the public's negative reaction.

*Left: 'Come On'/'I Want To Be Loved'*

*reveals much about the origin of the*

*Rolling Stones' music. Devoted to the*

*music of black Americans, the Stones*

*would continue to find inspiration in*

*rhythm and blues for the next 25 years.*

As 'Come On' slowly climbed the charts, Oldham vigorously promoted the group, and articles about the Stones began appearing in the papers regularly. Jagger and Oldham again clashed on the issue of suits, with Oldham finally relenting—all the while defending his previous position. From that point on Jagger began to take a more active part in the management of the group. Mick even insisted that Charlie let his hair grow longer so he wouldn't look so much like a jazz drummer.

The bad boy image that was so crucial for the Stones' professional life played havoc with their private lives. During this period, Mick Jagger was romantically involved with Chrissie Shrimpton, the younger sister of model Jean Shrimpton, but a steady girlfriend played no part in the Stones' image and Chrissie was relegated to

the background—a situation that would become the source of much anguish for her. To add to poor Chrissie's frustration, Mick privately promised her they would marry, while publicly asserting he had neither the plans nor the inclination to marry. Mick even went so far as to forbid Charlie Watts from marrying his fiancee, Shirley Shepherd. Charlie followed Mick's order for a time and then *secretly* married Shirley.

## THE FIRST TOUR

In the fall of 1963—from 29 September to 3 November—the Rolling Stones went on their first tour of Britain as part of a package with the Everly Brothers, Bo Diddley and Little Richard. The Stones

**Left: (from left to right) Charlie Watts, Keith Richards, Brian Jones, Bill Wyman and Mick Jagger, back stage on the set of Thank Your Lucky Stars. Brian and Bill don't seem to mind, but the others—Mick especially—are clearly fed up with posing for publicity stills. Jagger was on his way to becoming the dominant force in the band—off stage as well as on.**

were so awed to be appearing with Bo Diddley, one of their idols, that they dropped all the Bo Diddley numbers from their act for fear of his not liking their versions of his songs. As the tour was drawing to a close, the Stones released their second single. Although 'Come On' never made it above the lower levels of the charts, Oldham was pleased because at least the Stones were *on* the charts. Jagger was nevertheless disappointed and was determined that their next single would surpass the Beatles', who were by this time the toast of the town. The Beatles' latest single, 'From Me to You,' had shot to the top of the charts three weeks after its release. Ironically, the Beatles—actually only two of them, John Lennon and Paul McCartney—helped out with the Stones next single.

Lennon and McCartney had written the chorus of a song entitled 'I Wanna Be Your Man.' They played the incomplete song for the Stones and then immediately finished writing it in about five minutes. The song had the commercial sound that the Stones were looking for and was guaranteed to sell simply because it was penned by Lennon and McCartney. The Stones not only had a new single, they were inspired to try songwriting—since Lennon and McCartney made it seem so easy. 'I Wanna Be Your Man' backed with 'Stoned' was released on 1 November 1963.

'Stoned' was written by Nanker Phelge, a pseudonym for the Stones themselves. After recording 'I Wanna Be Your Man,' the Stones had only 30 minutes left of studio time to record the B-side. They began playing the usual Blues chord sequences while Mick chimed in at the appropriate moments. The end result was 'Stoned' (misspelled as 'Stones' on the first hundred pressings). The song was originally going to be released as the Stones' first single in the United States, but 'pressures were brought to bear to have it withdrawn instantly on moral grounds.'

All of the Stones, plus Ian Stewart, received equal shares in the songwriting royalties for 'Stoned,' but Mick and Keith would soon emerge as the official songwriters for the group. Though they lacked confidence at first, the pair was destined to be one of the great pop songwriting teams. In the tradition of the great songwriting teams of the first half of the century — Rodgers and Hart or the Gershwins — the teaming of Mick and Keith was a perfect marriage of personalities, with each one providing what the other one lacked. Jagger was the wordsmith, Richards the tunesmith. They were, however, standing in the shadow of Lennon and McCartney, and therefore Jagger and Richards — the songwriters — were overlooked.

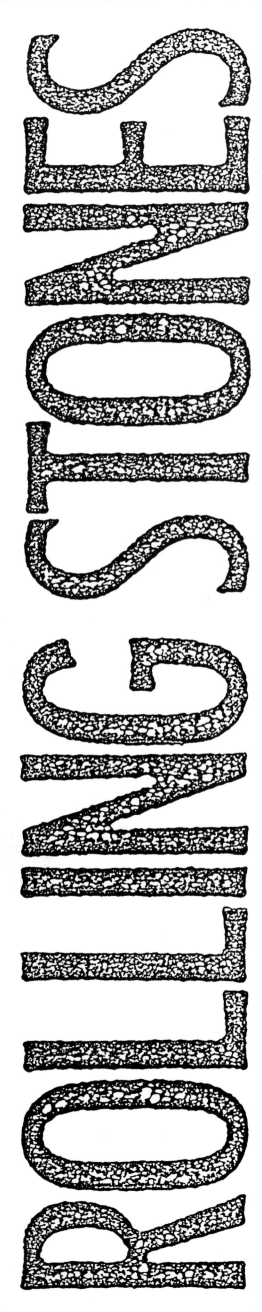
ROLLING STONES

# WOULD YOU LET YOUR DAUGHTER GO WITH A ROLLING STONE?

f 1963 was the year of the Beatles, 1964 was the year of the Rolling Stones. As the new year began the Stones made their first tour as headliners with the Ronettes. Within a month, they would have their first hit single and soon after their first album would knock the Beatles off the charts.

In January, the Stones released their first EP, *The Rolling Stones,* featuring four cover versions of American hits—'You Better Move On,' 'Money,' 'Bye, Bye Johnny' and 'Poison Ivy.' 'You Better Move On' was a standard from their club days and became a favorite on their many tours of Britain. The Stones set a record for touring in 1964, taking only 22 nights off the entire year. Bill Wyman told the press he was away from home so much that his own dog didn't recognize him and tried to bite him.

'Not Fade Away' hit the charts in February, eventually peaking at number three. The Stones were finally in a position to challenge the Beatles. Critics began making comparisons to the Beatles, which worked to the Stones' advantage since they were relatively unknown, whereas the Beatles were objects of adoration. 'Not Fade Away' was the first Stones single released in the United States, where it reached Number 48 on the charts.

In April 1964, the Stones released their first album in Great Britain. Sales hit a staggering 100,000 on first day of its release, smashing the previous record of 6000 set by the Beatles with the release of their first album, *Please Please Me,* and knocking the Beatles' latest album—*With the Beatles*—off the charts.

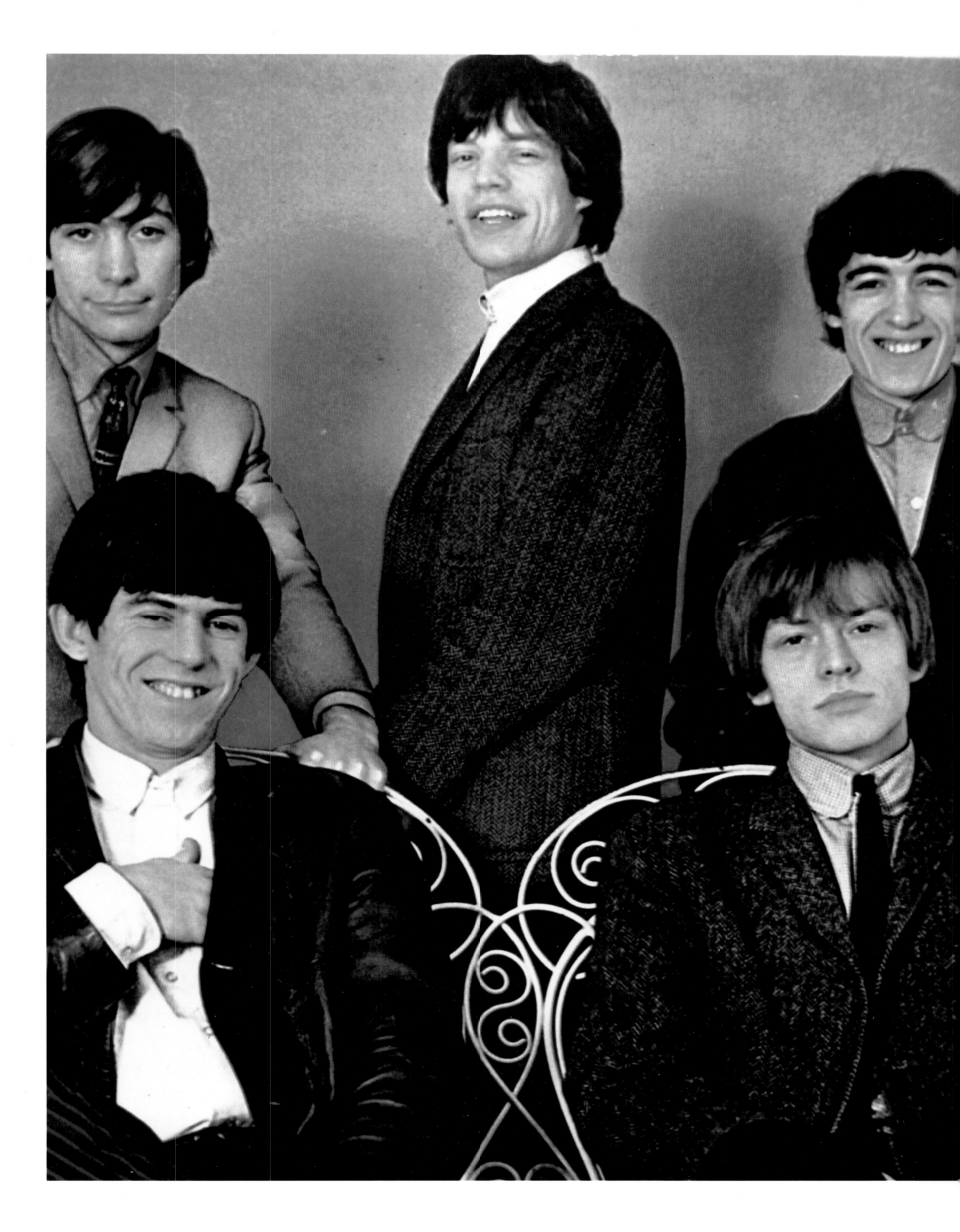

The album—known in the United States as *England's Newest Hit Makers*—has been described as '*the* classic album of white rock, because, like Presley's *Sun Sessions,* it was the first of its kind and it has the startled, breathless intensity of doing it for the first time.' 'Tell Me,' the first Jagger-Richards composition recorded by the Stones, is featured on the album.

The album cover itself was just as noteworthy, for it was the first time that an album had neither a title nor a name on the cover—just the penetrating gazes of the Stones, as photographed by David Bailey.

The album cover, with its moody, almost menacing, expressions, was just one part of Andrew Oldham's image making. From the outset, Andrew catered to the press and public's craving for scandalous news, spoonfeeding the papers with juicy tidbits of misinformation about 'the group that parents love to hate.' The *Melody Maker* headline of March 1964—'Would You Let Your Daughter Go With A Rolling Stone?'—had all the characteristics of Andrew's handiwork.

The Stones themselves helped nurture Andrew Oldham's carefully crafted image. Upon returning from their first North American tour, Keith Richards made sure the British press knew all about the collection of guns he had acquired while touring the United States. On 7 July 1964, Brian, Keith and Bill—'casually dressed and uninvited'—crashed the premiere of the Beatles' new movie, *A Hard Day's Night.*

## THE FIRST NORTH AMERICAN TOUR

On 2 June 1965, the Stones embarked on their first North American tour. In New York, the concerts turned into riots and teenage girls mobbed them, as they had the Beatles on their first tour of the United States two months earlier. Some girls were content to cut a swatch hair, while the bolder girls tried to make their way into their hotel rooms.

In Omaha, Nebraska, however, things were very different. Instead of screaming fans at the airport, they were met by a police escort—a publicity gimmick dreamed up by the promoter to drum up business. It didn't work. Only 637 people attended the concert, and of those at least 50 were police officers.

In Omaha, Keith also learned the bitter lesson that some people base their judgements on preconceived notions and not on what they see or hear. While sitting in the dressing room waiting to go on stage, the Stones were drinking whiskey and Coke out of paper cups. In walk the police, who demand to know what they are drinking. When told 'Whiskey,' the police ordered them to pour it down the drain. Keith happened to be drinking only Coke, and when he tried to explain, he found himself arguing with a .44 pistol.

It was almost as bad in Hollywood, where they appeared on Dean Martin's *Hollywood Palace.* Martin's idea of humor was to put down the band, so much so that they seriously considered walking off the stage. Typically, British bands would appear on *The Ed Sullivan Show* during their first tour of the States, but Sullivan refused to let the Stones appear because he perceived their image to be too rough for his Sunday night audience. Sullivan would soon relent. In less than six months the Stones would appear on his show during their second North American tour.

The public's reaction to the Stones was understandable. Most British groups had at least one hit record when they toured the United States for the first time. When the Stones first toured North America, 'Not Fade Away' was at the bottom of the charts, but the Stones saw the tour as a way to boost their record sales. The tour also gave them the chance to record the funky American sound that they loved. In England, no other group was doing what they were doing, so the studios and engineers simply lacked the expertise to record the kind of music the Stones were making.

A trip to Chess Records in Chicago—the studio from which young Mick and Keith had ordered their cherished blues and jazz

*In 1964, the Stones were on the road nonstop and the effects of the never-ending tour can be seen etched in their faces (below). In April of that year, they released their first album,* England's Newest Hit Makers, *which featured 'Tell Me,' the first composition by Mick and Keith (opposite page) to be recorded by the Stones.*

records—solved their problem. At Chess, the Stones cut their *Five by Five* EP as well as several other tracks that would appear on albums or as singles over the next six months.

Chicago gave the Stones the same kind of greeting they had received in New York. Their appearance at Chess Records turned a press conference into another riot.

On 28 June 1964, the Stones released 'It's All Over Now,' one of the songs recorded at Chess Records. The single zoomed to Number One on the British charts, giving the Stones their first number one single. A week later 'It's All Over Now' was released in the United States, where it reached number 25.

*On 7 August 1964, the Stones appeared on the television show Ready, Steady, Go! (right). Even though more than 20 policeman were lined up outside to hold back the mob of screaming girls, the unstoppable fans broke through the police line as the Stones ran for their limousine. As the chauffeur sped away, one of the car doors opened, knocking down a policeman and hitting a lamppost before the fans tore it off the hinges.*

On 24 October 1964, the Stones began their second tour of North America. By this time, *England's Newest Hit Makers* had made the Top Ten. Though still without a number one single in the United States, the Stones had a fanatical cult following, with membership in fan clubs up to 80,000 members.

In addition to their appearance on *The Ed Sullivan Show,* the Stones were the unquestioned stars of *The TAMI Show,* a documentary that featured the Beach Boys, the Supremes, Chuck Berry, Leslie Gore, Gerry and the Pacemakes and James Brown, among others. In between concerts and television shows, they found time to record half a dozen tracks at the RCA studios in Los Angeles.

Back in England, 'Little Red Rooster,' rush-released in September 1964, hit the charts at Number One — a feat accomplished previously only by Elvis, the Beatles, Cliff Richard and 'skiffle king' Lonnie Donnegan.

Mick and Keith were slowly becoming more confident of their songwriting abilities, but even though they were earning royalties for Marianne Faithfull's recording of 'As Tears Go By,' they were still reluctant to record one of their own compositions as the A side, unlike Lennon and McCartney, who had been recording their own compositions for the A side since the Beatles' second single. The Stones themselves didn't recognize their own potential.

Brian Jones, however, was feeling more confident and better about himself than he had in years. The Rolling Stones were successful beyond his wildest dreams, and he was convinced that within a year they would surpass the Beatles and become the biggest band in the world. The fan mail was pouring in, much of it addressed to Brian. Although he wouldn't publicly admit it, he considered himself the leader of the Stones. At the outset, everyone else had agreed that there would be no official leader, but the band had been his idea and he had been the one to bring everyone together. In the very beginning the press referred to Brian as the spokesman, but when the Stones toured America, the attention started to shift to Mick, and the thrill Brian was feeling now would turn to pain in the future.

As the year came to a close, the Stones were riding high, second in popularity to only the Beatles, according to a poll by the *New Musical Express.* They won the award for Best R & B Group and Best New Group. *Record Mirror*'s first annual pop music poll ranked the Stones *first,* with Mick Jagger receiving the most votes for the most popular individual in a group.

**Left:** ***Back in England after the first tour of the US in June 1964, the Stones performed at Oxford, the Queen's Hall in Leeds and various spots in London before heading to Glasgow, Scotland. Then it was on to The Hague in Holland, followed by a performance at the Olympia in Paris and finally back to the US for a second tour in October.***

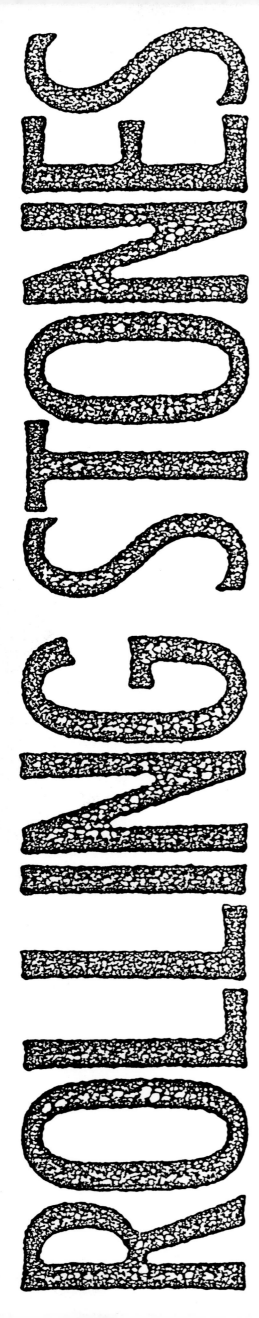

# SATISFACTION

I n their efforts to surpass the Beatles, the Stones continued their non-stop parade of cities, crisscrossing the British Isles, the Continent, the United States, even Australia. The touring paid off.

Their second British album—*The Rolling Stones No 2,* released in January 1965, was an immediate hit. Like their first album, the cover featured another surrealistic photograph by David Bailey. (The same cover appears on the *12 X 5* American LP.) The next month in the United States, the Stones released *The Rolling Stones Now!,* with tracks similar to those on *The Rolling Stones No 2.*

'The Last Time' backed with 'Play with Fire' (February 1965) shot to the top of the British charts in one week and became the Stones' first Top Ten hit in the United States. 'The Last Time' was the first Jagger-Richards composition to be released on the A side of a Stones single in Britain. It was—in Keith's words—'the first of our own songs that we really liked.' In the United States, the Stones had previously released two Jagger-Richards compositions on the A side: 'Tell Me' in June 1964 and 'Heart of Stone' in December 1964.

By the beginning of March, the Stones dominated the charts with the Number One single ('The Last Time'), EP (*Five by Five*) and album (*The Rolling Stones No 2*). 'The Last Time' eventually went gold, selling over a million copies worldwide.

In May 1965, the Stones released '(I Can't Get No) Satisfaction,' which they had recorded in Los Angeles during their last tour. The Stones first Number One hit in the United States, 'Satisfaction' cata-

pulted the Stones to fame. From Keith's opening fuzz-tone riffs, this anti-authoritarian anthem had its pulse on the emotions of the younger generation. It was one of the few songs written by Jagger and Richards that caught the mood of the times.

While on tour in Berlin in September 1965, 'Satisfaction' turned ugly. As a joke, during the instrumental break of the song, Jagger pranced around on stage, goose-stepping and throwing his arm out in a Nazi salute. The crowd went wild. Young boys rushed to the stage and were beaten back by police. After the concert, some of the boys remained inside, tearing out seats and breaking

*Mick, Bill and Charlie on TV (page 27) and relaxing off stage with the rest of the Stones (left) in 1964. As they toured the US in the fall of 1964, their 12 X 5 album (at top) was climbing the charts. The Stones kicked off 1965 with a quick trip to Ireland. Soon to follow were tours of Australia, New Zealand, the Far East, Scandinavia, West Germany and France. By the time they made their third tour of North America in May 1965, The Rolling Stones, Now! (above) had reached number nine on the charts.*

windows, while others ran outside and overturned cars and vandalized trains. Jagger had become more than just a rock star. A performer par excellence, he clearly had the ability to drive his audience into a frenzy. Ultimately, however, he would lose control.

The success of 'Satisfaction,' along with the assistance of Allen Klein, put the Stones in a strong bargaining position when their contract with Decca was up for renewal. Klein, an American, had made a name for himself by helping rock groups obtain back royalties that record companies had been withholding. His reputation was further established when Mickey Most, the manager of the

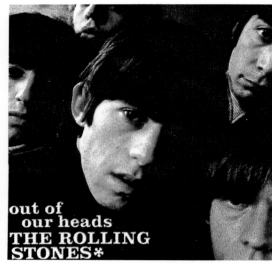

*Below: Half of the Jagger-Richards songwriting team. Though song-writing seemed a formidable task at first, by 1965 they were old hands at it. In January and February of 1965, the Stones convened at RCA Studios in Hollywood and recorded such classic Jagger-Richards compositions as 'The Last Time' and 'Play With Fire.' Years later Richards would remark 'Anyone who can play an instrument can write a song. . . . I had to come up with a No 1 hit every twelve weeks for about two years.'*

*Opposite page: The Rolling Stones, back in London.*

Animals and other groups, hired him as business manager. With his brash, New York style of negotiating, Klein was able to win huge advance royalties for Most's groups. Most sang Klein's praises to Andrew Oldham and Mick Jagger, and when Eric Easton's management contract with the Stones expired, it wasn't renewed. Klein would later become the Beatles' business manager.

Klein's negotiations with Decca Records produced terrific results for the Stones, making all of them rich. Prior to Klein's re-negotiations, the Stones had earned royalties of $375,000 from Decca and $236,000 from London Records in the United States. With Klein's assistance, they received a $7,000,000 advance. The days of collecting empty bottles for cash were long past.

'Satisfaction' was followed by the Dylanesque 'Get Off of My Cloud' (September 1965), another Number One hit. In the United States, 'Get Off of My Cloud' was included on *December's Children,* a collection of singles and tracks from English LPs and EPs. September 1965 also saw the release of *Out of Our Heads* in Britain. The American album, with different tracks, had been released the previous July and had already gone gold.

*Out of Our Heads* was the last Stones album in which the American release would differ substantially from the British one. The American version of *Out of Our Heads* had a greater impact than the British one because it featured a number of hit singles— 'Satisfaction,' 'Play With Fire' and 'The Last Time.'

## THE BAD BOYS OF ROCK AND ROLL

The Stones flaunted their bad boy image in what were sometimes rather amusing incidents. In March 1965, on their way home from a gig, the Stones stopped at a closed gas station to answer nature's call on the side of the wall. The local constabulary did not take kindly to their inventiveness and they were arrested for urinating in public.

Such high jinks made the Rolling Stones the darlings of the younger members of the aristocracy. They began traveling in circles with the who's who of society, such as Tara Browne, the heir to the Guinness fortune, and the Ormsby-Gores. It was rumored that 'Lady Jane' was about Jane Ormsby-Gore, but Mick publicly maintained that the song was based on a letter from Henry VIII to Jane Seymour and privately told Chrissie the song was written for her. Others, meanwhile, found the song laden with drug references.

While hobnobbing with high society, the Stones met Anita Pallenberg, a German model who would exert a considerable amount of influence over the Stones. Soon after Brian Jones met Anita, he left Linda Lawrence and their son, for her. Linda later showed up at his flat with their son, but Brian refused to let her in. He and Anita just stood at the window laughing at her. Soon after she moved in with Brian, Anita cut her hair and started wearing brightly colored silks. She was transformed into a twin of Brian, who seemed compelled to remake his women into his own image. Brian was just as willing to let Anita exert control over him. For a photograph, she dressed him up as a Nazi, standing with his foot on a Jewish-looking person, while she stood in the background laughing. The photograph was intended as a joke, and they failed to understand why people didn't think it was funny. They lived their lives as if they were king and queen, surrounded by their court—the upper crust of society who were behaving like groupies.

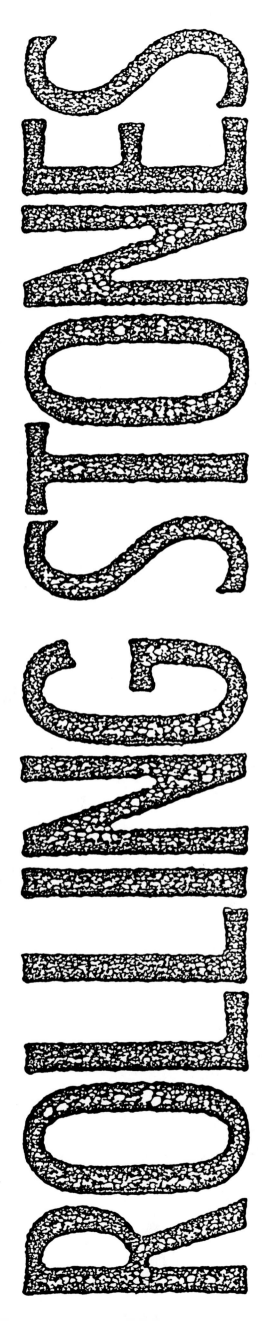

ROLLING STONES

# AS TEARS GO BY

**T**he Stones kicked off 1966 with an appearance on *The New Year Starts Here,* a television special on January 1. Within a few weeks, 'As Tears Go By,' released in the United States in December of the previous year, was high on the charts. One of the Stones' most unusual songs, 'As Tears Go By' was originally recorded by Marianne Faithfull.

Though she was a pop star in her own right in the mid-1960s, most people remember Marianne Faithfull as Mick Jagger's girl-friend. The daughter of a London University don and an Austrian baroness, Marianne Faithfull was just 17 when she first met Mick Jagger at a party, where he introduced himself by pouring a glass of champagne down the front of her blouse. Although many young women of the time would have been thrilled by Jagger's attention—crass though it was—Marianne was outraged by his behavior.

Andrew Oldham, the Stones' manager, saw Marianne at the same party where she met Jagger, and was convinced he could make her a star. As he had already proven, Oldham had a knack for finding the right person at the right time. At first reluctant to record a song, Marianne's curiosity finally propelled her into the limelight. She was about to graduate from St Joseph's Convent School in Reading and go on to university. Instead, she recorded Jagger and Richards' 'As Tears Go By.'

Marianne rejected Jagger's advances for quite some time. She married art dealer John Dunbar, and soon afterward they had

a son, Nicholas. Marianne's career conflicted with John's expectations for a wife and the mother of his child and the couple separated in October 1966. Meanwhile, Jagger's relationship with Chrissie Shrimpton, always volatile, was disintegrating. Soon after Mick broke up with Chrissie, Marianne Faithfull moved in with him. Mick, however, was not the first Stone with whom Marianne had been involved. 'I've slept with three of them,' she once said referring to her escapades with Brian Jones, Keith Richards and Mick Jagger, 'and decided the singer was the best.'

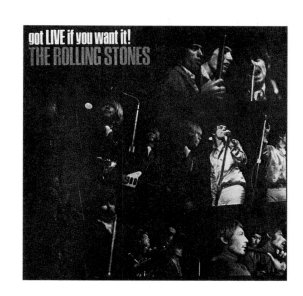

About the time he became involved with Marianne, Jagger purchased a Georgian town house in Cheyne Walk, on the banks of the Thames. As lady of the house, it was Marianne's task to turn the house into a Mick's dream world, decorating it with antiques, lush Oriental rugs and tapestries. She bought an antique crystal chandelier for $15,000, a sum which absolutely delighted Jagger. He loved the idea that she had spent an outrageous sum of money on a light fixture.

Mick was not the sort to sit contentedly at home for long. Mick, Marianne and her son Nicholas would dash off to spend a few days with Keith at Redlands, or with Charlie and Shirley at their 700-year-old home in Sussex. So great was his need to be on the move that he purchased yet another home, this time an Elizabethan manor outside Newbury. The estate—Stargroves—which included forty acres of green, wooded hills, had been Cromwell's lodging after the Second Battle of Newbury in 1644. Faced with two centuries' worth of decay, Mick was nonetheless determined to restore Stargroves to its original condition.

During her years with Jagger, Marianne moved from pop star to actress. In 1968, she starred with Alain Delon in the French film *The Girl on the Motorcycle.* The following year she appeared in Chekhov's *Three Sisters* at the Royal Theatre in London. She also played Ophelia in a film production of *Hamlet.*

## BACK IN THE STUDIO

In February 1966 the Stones released '19th Nervous Breakdown.' By this time all the Stones' singles were topping the charts, and this one was no exception. In Britain, the single was backed with 'As Tears Go By,' and in the United States by 'Sad Day.'

Three albums—all 'firsts' in their own way—would be released before the year's end. In March 1966, the Stones released their first greatest hits album—*Big Hits (High Tide and Green Grass).* In November 1966, the Stones released *Got Live If You Want It,* their first live album.

**Page 33:** *The Rolling Stones in June 1966. Notice that Brian Jones has branched out from the guitar.*

**Opposite page:** *Marianne Faithfull recorded the Stones' 'As Tears Go By' in 1964, when she was 18. Though she had a few other hits, she was better known as Mick Jagger's girl friend than as a singer. About 1966 she focused her energies on acting, but started recording again in the late 1970s. This photo was taken in the post-Jagger years while she was working on re-establishing her career as a singer.*

The Stone's first album of all original compositions—*Aftermath*—came out in June 1966, its impact lessened by the simultaneous release of the Beatles' *Revolver* and Bob Dylan's *Blonde on Blonde. Aftermath* revealed the scope and versatility of the Jagger-Richards song-writing team. In addition to the Elizabethan ballad 'Lady Jane,' the album included blues ('Going Home') and two songs that were destined to become rock and roll classics—'Paint It, Black' and 'Under My Thumb.'

In January 1967 the Stones appeared again on *The Ed Sullivan Show* in their historic performance of 'Let's Spend the Night Together.' The show's censors found the song's lyrics objectionable and Jagger was asked to change the words to 'Let's spend some time together.' Although one story says that the lines were actually censored, Jagger maintains that he mumbled when he came to

*The album* Aftermath *(above) featured 'Paint It, Black,' for which* **Brian Jones** *(forefront of the photo at left) learned the sitar, and learned it well. Charlie Watts later recalled that Brian spent hours learning how to play the instrument for the song, but never played it again.*

**Opposite page:** *The Rolling Stones demonstrating the icy stares and malevolent scowls that became their trademark.*

the words in question. Those who saw the show claim he sang 'some time.'

January 1967 saw the release of *Between the Buttons.* Like *Aftermath,* it highlighted the versatility of Jagger and Richards as songwriters. Not only does the album have a variety of songs, but the songs themselves are rich and unusual. One technique the Stones used to create variety within a song was to change the tempo, as in 'Let's Spend the Night Together' and 'Ruby Tuesday.' The latter song benefitted as well from Brian Jones' flute. He also played the marimbas on 'Yesterday's Papers,' the organ on 'She Smiled Sweetly' and the piano on 'Cool, Calm and Collected.'

The Stones were not the only group experimenting with different musical instruments. George Harrison had played the sitar on 'Norwegian Wood' on the Beatles' *Rubber Soul* (1965) and the Beatles' *Revolver* (1966) featured a host of unusual instruments. As with the Beatles, this time would later be regarded as one the Stones' most successful periods of musical experimentation.

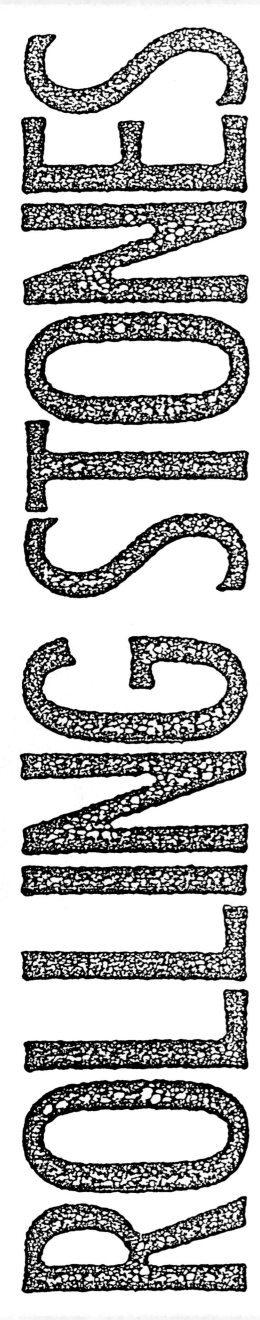

# THE RAID AT REDLANDS

On 12 February 1967, the local police appeared on the doorstep of Redlands, Keith Richards's mansion, with a search warrant. Inside, watching television to the sound of The Who, were Keith, Mick, Marianne Faithfull and a few guests. The group was slowly coming down from an acid trip that had started early that day. Much to the delight of the press, Marianne Faithfull was clad in only a fur rug. After a day of hiking, she had taken a bath and had wrapped herself up in the rug to avoid having to put on her dirty clothes.

After searching the place, the police confiscated four pep pills that Mick and Marianne had legally purchased in Italy. They also found a small amount of hash that actually belonged to some of the guests, but they had ignored a suitcase belonging to Henry Schneiderman that contained every drug imaginable. Though the police were clearly novices at drug searches, it became apparent that their goal was to nail Mick and Keith. When the police left, they told Keith he would be held responsible if it was determined that any of the drugs had been used on his property.

On 10 May 1967, Mick and Keith, along with Robert Fraser, who had been one of the guests at Redlands, appeared at the local court in Chichester for the preliminary hearing. Mick was charged with the possession of four amphetamine tablets without authorization, Keith was charged with permitting his home to be used for smoking illegal substances, and Robert Fraser with illegal posses-

sion of heroin. The charges against Fraser were the most serious, and Mick and Keith believed that the trial would be routine and they would win the case.

While the court was in recess, Keith called Brian's flat to say they would soon be on their way to London. Anita told him that the police had arrested Brian. The timing of Brian's arrest coincided too perfectly with the hearing for it to be mere coincidence. To those involved, it now seemed clear that the police were out to get the Stones.

A month later Mick was sentenced to three months imprisonment and 100 pounds costs. Keith's sentence was rougher: one year and five hundred pounds cost. Mick was taken to Brixton Prison and Keith to Wormwood Scrubs, a 150-year old prison. His belt was taken away so that he would not hang himself and he was given only a blunt spoon because a knife and fork could be honed into a weapon. After two days, they were each granted bail of $17,000 and released pending appeal of their conviction.

The Stones carefully crafted bad boy image and Oldham's slogan—the group that parents love to hate—had come back to haunt them tenfold. The drug bust gave the press and the public a concrete reason to disapprove of the Stones. Given the circumstances of the arrest—overlooking drugs that belonged to the guests, the timing of Brian's arrest—it now seems certain that those in authority wanted to pin a drug rap on the Rolling Stones. They were guilty, but the punishment did not fit the crime. Even the conservative *Times* came to Mick and Keith's defense. Following their sentencing, the *Times* ran an editorial criticizing the court's handling of the case.

While their lawyers had been preparing for the hearing, life went on as usual for the Rolling Stones. On 25 March 1967, the band left England for a brief tour of the Continent. The Stones hadn't played Europe for a year and in every city their appearance was greeted with riots and mass hysteria. In Vienna, over 150 fans were arrested after smoke bombs were thrown in a 14,000-

**Page 35:** *Mick Jagger was born to the stage. Even back in the days at the Crawdaddy Club, he had the power to mesmerize an audience.*

**Left:** *The Stones, during their psychedelic phase.*

Opposite page: *The Stones, minus Bill Wyman, about a month before the infamous raid at Redlands.*

*Though generally panned by the critics,* Their Satanic Majesties Request *(at bottom) had a hit single with 'She's a Rainbow.'* Satanic Majesties *also featured 'In Another Land,' a Bill Wyman song with Bill doing the lead vocals, and '2000 Light Years From Home,' which would resurface in concert 22 years later during the Stones' Steel Wheels tour.*

seat stadium. In Orebro, Sweden, fans threw bottles, firecrackers and chairs when police started beating girls over the head with truncheons. The Stones were forced to flee the concert hall.

In Warsaw, the police used teargas, batons and a water cannon to break up an angry mob. The Stones' had never played in Eastern Europe and fans were upset because most of the best tickets had been given to the leaders of the Communist Party. Shortly after the concert began, Keith stopped the band from playing and ordered the people down in front—those with the diamonds and the pearls—to move out of their seats and let the real fans come down. Most of the people did move to the back and the true Stones fans rushed forward.

In addition to riots—which to Mick were simply part of performing—the Stones were subjected to thorough searches by the custom officials at the airports throughout Europe. Officials at Orly Airport told Mick that he had been placed on an International Red List of suspected narcotics smugglers.

## THEIR SATANIC MAJESTIES REQUEST

After returning from the tour, with less than a month remaining before the preliminary hearing, the Stones turned their energies to the studio. The album was to be called *Her Satanic Majesties Request*—a none too subtle reference to the Queen (from the first line in the front of British passports 'Her Britannic Majesty's...Request and requires...') Under pressure from Decca, the name was finally changed to *Their Satanic Majesties Request*.

The album, which is unequivocally regarded as the Stones' worst effort, was their entry into psychedelic music. Known also as 'acid rock' or the 'San Francisco sound,' psychedelic music supposedly recreated the 'trips' induced by hallucinogenic drugs, such as LSD (lysergic acid diethylamide, or acid, as it was commonly known). Borrowing from the music of India and the Middle East, psychedelic music used a wide range of electronic effects.

The Stones were masters at their own kind of rhythm and blues-based rock and roll, but this venture into a new kind of music was one experiment that failed miserably. Mick later defended the album, declaring that it 'was the mood of the times.' But many fans wondered if the Stones were serious. Musically, they were not as flexible or as electric as the Beatles, nor did they have the production skills to smooth out the rough spots, as George Martin did for the Beatles' *Sgt Pepper.*

It was an era when drug use was widespread as well as accepted—even encouraged—among some segments of the

population. Drugs were trendy and all the artists—musicians, writers, photographers, designers—saw drugs as a way to enhance their creativity. The Beatles' most complex albums— *Rubber Soul, Revolver* and *Sgt Pepper's Lonely Hearts Club Band*—were created when they were experimenting with LSD.

Brian was the first of the Stones to try LSD. Shortly after he and Anita moved in together, they decided to experiment, thinking the experience would be much like smoking pot. Brian especially used drugs to 'unlock the songs that were trapped inside his head.' For a brief time, Brian was enormously creative. The acid made it seem that anything was possible. Keith witnessed the energy, and could see that Brian and Anita were having incredible visions and wanted to join them on their trips. He moved in with them, tried acid and began working with them. 'Ruby Tuesday' was one of Brian and Keith's combined efforts. Eventually, however, Brian fell deeper and deeper into the abyss of drug use. When acid started to fail to release the music he still heard inside his head, the answer was to try more drugs.

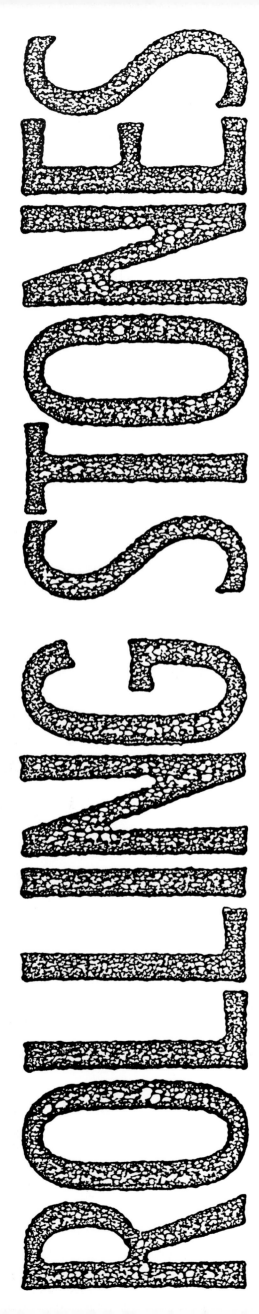

ROLLING STONES

# PLEASE ALLOW ME TO INTRODUCE MYSELF

One venture into psychedelia was enough for the Rolling Stones. When they got together in the studio in the spring of 1968, they got down to business and recorded what has been dubbed by many rock critics as the 'quintessential rock and roll song'—'Jumpin' Jack Flash.' More than twenty years later Keith Richards would call 'Jumpin Jack Flash' a 'killer song. You'd have to have all your limbs cut off before you'd stop playing it. They could be asking me, "Any last words? Want a cig? A blindfold?" And I'd say, "No, just let me play Jumpin' Jack Flash one more time." In direct contrast to the musical debacle that was *Their Satanic Majesties Request,* the Stone's next album—*Beggar's Banquet*—was heralded as their best effort yet. The album (released in November 1968) returned to their blues roots, delivering hard and sensuous rock and roll. The music demonstrated the Stones' ability to take an earlier form of music and make it stronger. It was what rock and roll was all about—music that gave voice to restless, rebellious youth.

The opening cut—'Sympathy for the Devil'—was inspired by *The Master and Margarita* by Mikhail Bulgakov. The novel, which is an allegory of the struggles between good and evil, tells the story of Satan in Moscow of the 1930s. In a world gone mad, Satan walks around saying 'Permit me to introduce myself.' Mick, of course, immortalized those words in the opening of 'Sympathy for the Devil': 'Please allow me to introduce myself…'

**Page 45 and above:** *A bearded Mick Jagger as Ned Kelly, in the movie of the same name.* **Right:** *Mick in* Performance.

Filmed in December 1968, under the direction of Michael Lindsay-Hogg, the Rolling Stones' Rock and Roll Circus *was planned as a television special. The special was never shown, but various bootleg recordings of the musical performances have made it legendary.*

**Opposite page, all:** *Keith Richards on bass, John Lennon, Eric Clapton on guitar and Mitch Mitchell on drums perform John's 'Yer Blues.'*

*Beggar's Banquet* also contains 'Street Fighting Man,' which was written in response to the Paris student riots of 1968 — the 'Second French Revolution.' An anthem for revolution, it also expresses Jagger's personal disappointment that he cannot be a part of that revolution. Because it was feared that the song would incite riots, it received limited air play in Great Britain and was banned in the United States.

Like *Their Satanic Majesties Request, Beggar's Banquet* was produced under a cloud of controversy. The album's release was delayed for five months over a debate surrounding photos for the album cover, which showed a lavatory wall covered with graffiti. Decca refused to distribute the album with that photo, and Mick and Keith refused to allow its release without the jacket they had selected. In the end, Decca won. Wanting to rectify the mistake they had made with their last album, the Stones were anxious to give their fans hard driving rock and roll. Moreover, the Stones freely admitted they agreed to Decca's demands because they needed the money. *Beggar's Banquet* was released in December with a plain cover — an invitation written in elegant script.

## MICK, THE MOVIE STAR

In concert, as he prances about the stage, Mick is the consummate performer, so it is only natural that he would turn to acting. After *Beggar's Banquet* was completed, Mick began rehearsing for his first acting part — the leading role in *Performance.* Directed by Donald Cammell and Nicholas Roeg, the movie tells the story of a reclusive rock star (Jagger) and a gangster. The movie focuses on the seamy side of life and the decadent, drugged world of the film was thought by many to parallel the world of the Stones themselves. After the movie was completed, Warner Bros found it too sor-

did and delayed its release for two years. Anita Pallenberg also starred in the film, and it was rumored that she and Mick had a brief off-screen affair.

In 1969, Mick starred in a second film, *Ned Kelly,* in which he played the title role, a character in the Robin Hood tradition. Marianne Faithfull was to be his costar, but she took an overdose of pills and went into a coma. When she regained consciousness, she began treatment for heroin addiction.

Her years with Mick Jagger had been happiness tempered with trauma. While Mick was preparing for his role in *Performance,* she discovered she was pregnant with Mick's child. The pillars of society were shocked when it was announced that the couple had no plans to marry. As an additional slap in the face to convention, Marianne was still married to John Dunbar. The pregnancy was a difficult one and Marianne's doctor ordered her to rest. The happiness she had felt when she learned she was pregnant was replaced by a growing sense of frustration. Like Chrissie Shrimpton before her, Marianne was feeling trapped and confused by the relationship and relied heavily on cocaine to ease her boredom. In her seventh month of pregnancy, Marianne had a miscarriage.

Coke would eventually give way to heroin, and Marianne, who hated needles, could always count on a friend to shoot her up. She began to feel like a victim of Mick Jagger's fame.

Soon after the miscarriage, Mick and Marianne decided to take a vacation to South America with Keith. Keith fueled the gossip columns with his remark that they were going to meet a magician, one who practiced both white and black magic. Coming on the tails of 'Sympathy for the Devil,' Keith's little white lie caused people to speculate that the Stones were becoming involved in black magic. By now the Stones were masters of the ironic put-down, but all too often people missed the point. Some people—those who were out of touch with reality—started associating Jagger with Lucifer and were convinced he would create a worldwide revolution.

The unrepentant bad boy image was one the Stones had culti-vated since their early years. They deliberately scowled while per-forming, and an early publicity still showed them tilting over a baby carriage. Andrew Oldham cast them in the mold of the characters from Anthony Burgess' *Clockwork Orange.* Eventually the bad boy image became exaggerated, and people began to find refer-ences to black magic in their work. On the cover of *Between the Buttons,* a black cat can be seen around the buttons of Charlie Watts' jacket, and *Their Satanic Majesties Request* is an obvious reference. Though it was a deliberate affectation, their demonic associations would come to haunt them with 'Sympathy for the Devil.'

**Above:** *The Stones' original choice for the sleeve for* **Beggar's Banquet.** *Twenty years later London Records relented and re-released the album with its controversial cover.*

**Left and opposite page:** *The bad boys of rock and roll take a brief repast from their demanding schedule. So how come they don't look relaxed?*

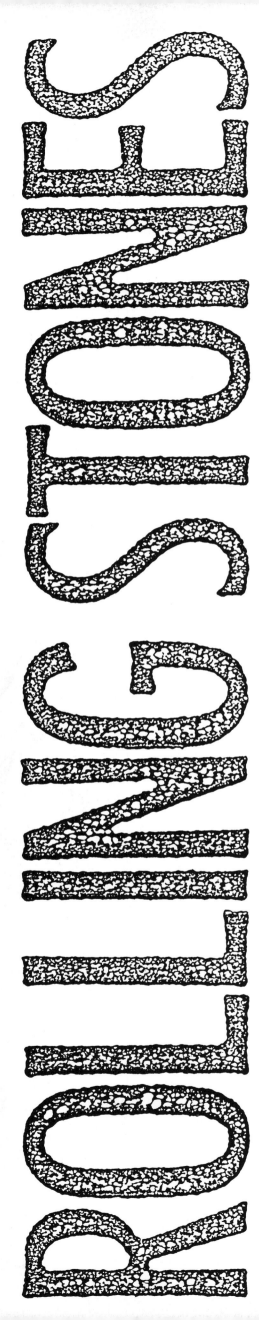

# THE DEATH OF BRIAN JONES

I used to play my guitar as a kid
wishing I could be like him
But today I changed my mind I
decided that I that I don't want to die
But it was a normal day for Brian
Rock and roll's that way
It was a normal day for Brian
A man who died every day'

—Pete Townsend

Brian Jones lived the wild life that the press attributed to all the Stones, but he was a much more fragile individual. The nonstop touring from 1963 to 1966 had drained him, more so than the other Stones. Following the first drug bust in 1967, Mick and Keith were able to dismiss their legal entanglements from their minds and concentrate on putting *Their Satanic Majesties Request* together, but not all the Stones could leave their troubles behind them. Brian suffered under the combined pressure of his arrest and the 1967 European tour. Even the adulation of his fans exhausted him.

In addition, he had recently endured severe personal losses. His good friend Tara Browne, one of the few people with whom Brian could talk without being told he was paranoid, had been killed in an automobile accident.

Then Anita left him for Keith. The betrayal by one of his closest friends, coupled with the loss of Anita, played a major role in the decline and fall of Brian Jones. She left him when he needed her the most. When LSD began to fail him, Brian turned to other drugs—

mandrax, desbutal, amphetamines and barbiturates. Though some were legal, the combination was lethal. His body and mind slowly being destroyed by drugs, he was hospitalized to clean out his system. While Brian was in the hospital, Anita left him for Keith. She came back to him briefly, but the break would soon be final. The last thing Brian needed in April 1967 was to spend time in the studio with Keith. To make matters worse, Anita put in an occasional appearance. As an escape, Brian spent much of the time stoned out of his mind, asleep on the studio floor while the rest of the Stones were trying to record.

Perhaps if he had liked the music on which they were working, he could have found the drive he needed to go on, but that was just one more thing that was wrong with life then. The Stones were working on *Their Satanic Majesties Request.* Brian hated the music they were creating. He felt it was a crass commercial attempt to

**Page 52:** *Brian Jones, circa 1963, with his Greisch guitar. He also played harmonica, organ, marimba, sitar, dulcimer, recorder, bells, saxophone, harpsichord and Mellotron.*

**Right:** *Brian, with Bill and Charlie, during an early television performance.*

**Opposite page:** *An actress, a model — she was even accused of being a witch, but whatever she was, Anita Pallenberg was definitely a heartbreaker. Brian Jones never got over her leaving him for his best friend, Keith Richards.*

cash in on the current psychedelic craze. To his mind, the psychedelic 'trash' couldn't even be called music. It may have seemed to Brian that the album was also an attempt to force him out of the group.

Brian's reaction to the music is ironic given his fascination with unusual instruments and his interest in the Middle East. In his travels to Morocco, Brian had become enraptured with the local musicians. His recordings of their pipes and drums were released in 1971 as *Brian Jones Presents the Pipes of Pan in Jajouka*.

Brian had been unhappy for some time and had talked about leaving the group before, but he didn't want to spend the rest of his life as just an ex-Rolling Stone. Brian's place of importance had gradually been overshadowed by Mick. While the Stones had no official leader, the press and the public alike now acknowledged Mick as the leader of the band. Though never openly adversarial, at times the relationship between Mick and Brian was strained to the point where they accused those around them of choosing sides. Furthermore, Mick and Keith ruled songwriting. Brian, as well as Bill Wyman, was writing songs, but by and large only Jagger-Richards compositions were being recorded.

Everyone certainly recognized Brian's musical abilities. His talents had a far greater range than any of the other Stones'. He instinctively knew what musical instrument would supply just the right harmony. When Brian was at the height of his creative energies, he could be seen dashing around the studio—playing harp, electric or acoustic guitar, dulcimer, mellotron, organ. Whatever was needed, Brian could provide it.

By the end of 1967, the album was completed and Brian's trial was over, but another rift in the group had been created because Mick wanted to tour South America and Japan but Brian's conviction prohibited him from leaving the country. Brian had been convicted of possession of cannabis and sentenced to nine months in jail. In November, the Court of Appeals, acting on medical advice, changed the sentence to a fine of 1000 pounds and three years probation. As an additional part of the sentence, Brian was required to seek medical attention.

Within two days, Brian had collapsed and was rushed to the hospital. After an hour he was released, his doctor reassuring the press that nothing was wrong: Brian was tired and overworked. The truth is that Brian was once again flying high on acid and coke. While at a nightclub, he had jumped on stage with the band and started playing the string bass—with his boots—until the bass splintered, but Brian didn't notice that the bass was ruined. He just kept on playing an instrument that was no longer there.

Brian was caught in the web of drug abuse. Unable to function, his mental condition suffered further at the hands of the police. Brian had become a target for the authorities, much as Lenny Bruce had earlier in the States. On 21 May 1968, Brian was arrested a second time for possession of drugs. He had just returned from a trip to the country when Les Perrin, the Stones' publicist, phoned Brian to say that he had just received a tip that the police were on their way to raid Brian's flat. Unconcerned, Brian assured Les that the police would not find anything. He had not stopped using drugs—and in fact was using them more heavily—but was careful to keep his flat drug free. He never carried drugs with him and only used them at friends'.

Shortly after Les Perrin's call, the police arrived. Brian ignored their knocking, and after ten minutes they climbed through an open window. Armed with a warrant, they searched Brian's flat and soon discovered what they were looking for—a ball of blue yarn, which presumably contained Brian's stash of drugs. At the police station, they finally showed Brian a chunk of hashish and charged him with possession. Brian insisted that he had been framed, that the police had planted the hashish as well as the yarn.

Four months later the case went to trial. Judge Seaton reminded the jurors that the evidence was circumstantial. The defense had pointed out that Brian could easily have flushed the 'evidence' down the toilet in the 10 minutes before the police entered his flat. In 45 minutes the jury reached a verdict: guilty. Given the judge's comments, the verdict was a complete surprise. The judge, however, went easy on him. He was fined 50 pounds and 100 guineas court costs, and the judge cautioned him to watch his step. But the damage had already been done. For all practical purposes, Brian was no longer a Rolling Stone.

When the Stones met in the studio to work on *Beggar's Banquet,* Brian once again was unable to work. Ironically, it was the bluesy sort of music he loved. 'Stray Cat Blues' could have come straight out of one Brian's fantasies. Instead of getting into the music, Brian would show up late at the studio and either fall asleep in a corner or sit on a chair and cry quietly into a microphone. The rest of the Stones finally decided that the best way to handle Brian was to send him off into another room—even on those rare days when he was feeling fine. The end result is that Brian did not play a single note of *Beggar's Banquet.* Keith overdubbed on three guitars, and several other musicians were brought in to cover for Brian.

The situation was unchanged in early 1969 when the Stones started *Let It Bleed.* This time there was no pretense that Brian Jones was part of the Rolling Stones. The Stones started work in the studio without him. The band was planning to go on tour that year and Brian couldn't go with them. That, of course, was just a convenient reason to finally make the break. Brian hadn't been a Stone for some time.

Mick and Keith knew that they had to break the news to him so they drove down to Redlands, Keith's mansion where Brian was staying while his home was being renovated. They all agreed that the press needed a story. Brian was ambivalent about the reason—whatever Mick and Keith wanted to say was fine. They decided to announce that Brian and the Stones 'could no longer see eye to eye' on their music. In the meantime, Jagger had been courting Mick Taylor of John Mayall's Bluesbreakers to replace Brian. The public's reaction to Brian's departure was one of disbelief. To the fans he was a mythic figure who could not possibly be replaced. More than any other Stone, except perhaps Jagger, he

**Opposite page:** *The Rolling Stones in January 1967, before Brian Jones began to feel the effects of too many drugs and too much harassment from the police. By the time the Stones started working on* **Let It Bleed** *(above) in early 1969, Brian was a Stone in name only.* **At top: Brian Jones and Helen Jones.**

**Below:** *The back cover for* Let It Bleed. **Right:** *Brian Jones, about a year before his death, and in a contemplative mood (opposite page). The eyes reveal a being too fragile for the excessive life of a Rolling Stone.*

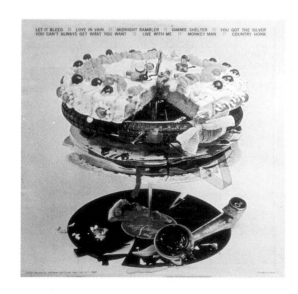

epitomized what the Rolling Stones were all about—even though he had not participated in any group efforts for a while.

Though he was despondent over his dismissal from the Stones, Brian seemed to be rebounding. He had cut back on drugs and was excited about remodeling his new home—Cotchford Farm. The place had once belonged to AA Milne, and Brian found peace in the whimsical stone figures of Pooh, Piglet and Christopher Robin that were scattered about the grounds. He had also been talking with his old friend Alex Korner, founder of Blues Incorporated—the band Brian had played in what seemed like so many years ago. Brian was eager to get back to the music he played before and talked of forming a band of his own

On 3 July 1969 Brian Jones was found dead at the bottom of his swimming pool.

The circumstances surrounding Brian's death are hazy. One version reports that Brian had gone for a midnight swim and was left alone briefly when his girl friend, Anna Wohlin, went into the house to answer the phone. When she returned he was unconscious. Another version has it that a friend, Frank Thorogood, had been watching him swim and when he felt certain that Brian was sober enough to swim, he went into the house for a cigarette. Some people speculated that Brian had had an asthma attack, but the coroner found no evidence of one. What he did find was a liver and heart ravaged by the excesses of alcohol and drugs. The official cause of death was listed as 'death by misadventure.'

The Stones were scheduled to perform at a free concert at London's Hyde Park two days after Brian's death. After debating whether to go ahead with the show, the Stones decided to dedicate the concert to Brian. As a memorial to Brian, Jagger read Shelly's *Adonais,* a romantic poem about early death. When Mick was finished reading, hundreds of white butterflies were released. The crowd went wild even though the band was somewhat rusty and even though they had just fired the man they were memorializing.

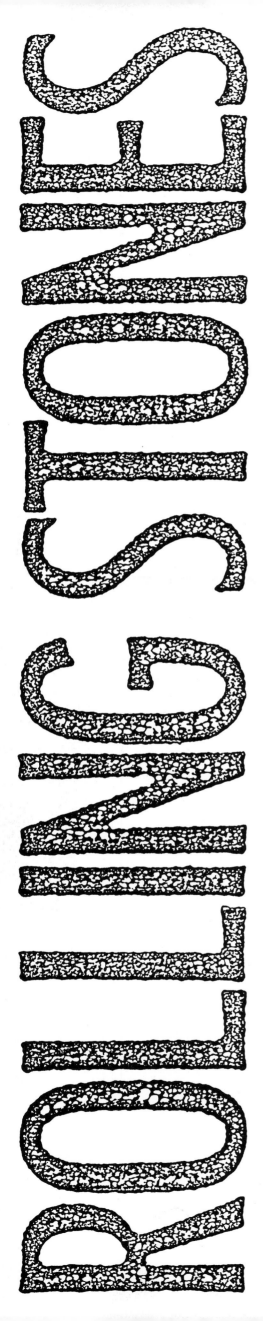

ROLLING STONES

# ALTAMONT

The Stones had stopped touring in the spring of 1967 and the Hyde Park concert gave them the opportunity to rehearse for their upcoming tour. It also marked Mick Taylor's debut as a Rolling Stone. Taylor, an innocent 20-year-old, was a good musician but he didn't quite fit the image of a Rolling Stone. A vegetarian and non-drinker, Taylor had grown musically frustrated with Mayall's band.

The release of *Let It Bleed* was timed to coincide with the start of the first major tour in three years since the Beatles and the Stones had stopped touring. Most people saw the title as a sardonic reply to the Beatles' *Let It Be,* but the Stones themselves maintain that the title is nothing more than a line from a song. Made in the blues tradition, like *Beggar's Banquet,* this album is the Stones at their best. They play their old, familiar roles of swaggering studs and evil demons. To some the Stones are evil personified and Jagger is Lucifer, but from the Stones' point of view all they are trying to say is that there is evil in the world. The album opens with 'Midnight Rambler,' a raw, bluesy number that pays homage to a rapist. In concert, Mick, on his knees, emphasizes the sexual overtones of the song by holding the microphone between his legs as he sings. As the song progresses he takes off his belt and whips the stage.

The mood established with 'Midnight Rambler' continues throughout most of the album. The piercing voice of Mary Clayton helps Mick bring the fear and desperation of 'Gimme Shelter' to a climax, while the London Bach Choir provides an interesting

*Page 59: Mick Jagger in Jean-Luc Godard's* Sympathy For The Devil. *The semi-documentary captured the Stones, including Brian, recording that infamous song.* Right: *Mick Taylor—the replacement for Brian Jones. He left the Stones five years later so that he would not meet the same fate as Brian.*

*Opposite page, below: Taylor, Jagger and one of their promoters at the press conference at the Beverly Wilshire Hotel in Los Angeles announcing their 1969 tour. The 13-city, 18-show tour opened at the Los Angles Forum on 8 November.*

*Opposite page, above: Bill Wyman, at the same press conference.*

contrast to the frustration heard in 'You Can't Always Get What You Want.' *Let It Bleed* also contains the surprisingly good country version of 'Honky Tonk Women'—'Country Honk.' The only track not written by the Stones is 'Love In Vain,' a ballad by bluesman Robert Johnson.

The crowds across America were eager to see the Stones again, despite the then-outrageous price of $12.50 a ticket. The Stones were their demonic selves and Mick especially was dressed the part in tight black pants with silver studs up the sides, a black jersey with a beige horseshoe—the astrological symbol for Leo, his sign—emblazoned across the front, a jeweled belt and a long red scarf.

The Stones decided to conclude the tour with a free concert in Golden Gate Park in San Francisco, the city where free concerts began. It would be a West Coast Woodstock memorialized in film. Dreams are not so easy to plan, and the group ran into problems with the site for a concert. After the City of San Francisco refused to issue a permit, the concert was scheduled for Sears Point Raceway,

30 miles north of the city. Then that locale fell through. Twenty hours before the concert was scheduled to begin the Stones announced it would take place at Altamont, 30 miles east of San Francisco.

Rock impresario Bill Graham was outraged. There was no way the site could be readied in time for the crowd that was expected. At the suggestion of the Grateful Dead (a San Francisco-based psychedelic band, which even today has a large, cult-like following), the Stones hired Hell's Angels as security. The Hell's Angels had provided security for the Hyde Park concert following Brian's death, but the London Angels were a tamer crew than their California counterparts. Cynics later said the Hell's Angels were hired not so much for protection as to complement the Stones' Satanic image.

According to those who read the stars, it was destined to be a bad day, one filled with violence and chaos. Santana, the lead band, kicked off two hours late. As the Jefferson Airplane began their set, a fight broke out on stage between a Hell's Angel and a lone black man. Several Angels leapt on stage to beat him with pool cues. When Marty Balin of the Airplane tried to stop the beating he was knocked unconscious by an Angel. Meanwhile, doctors in the medical tent were busy treating dozens of kids 'tripping out on bad acid.'

The situation calmed down during the performance of the Flying Burrito Brothers, but the Angels ruled again while Crosby, Stills, Nash and Young played. They finished their act and the audience began waiting for the Stones, but the wait dragged on for over 90 minutes. A rumor circulated through the crowd that Jagger was waiting for darkness to fall to heighten the drama of his entrance.

**Above:** *Keith and Charlie at the Beverly Wilshire. Los Angeles was in a fever pitch. Groupies hung out at the Stones' official headquarters in the Hollywood Hills, while across town in a more secluded location, the Stones set up camp with their chauffeurs, cooks and bodyguards.*

Finally, Mick leapt into 'Jumpin' Jack Flash,' his orange and black cape glowing under the lights. He tried to dance but the stage was filled with people. They ignored his pleas to move back. For once, Jagger was not in control—he had not been the one to incite the crowd into a frenzy. He was overwhelmed by circumstances. As he began 'Sympathy for the Devil,' a nude woman climbed on stage. Five Angels rushed to beat her off the stage and Jagger stopped the song, sarcastically pointing out that one Angel should be able to handle her. The song was going badly by now, but still Jagger sang on. Suddenly he stopped. Someone in the crowd had a gun, pointed directly at Jagger.

The man with the gun disappeared into the crowd. The man, who was black, had been standing with his white girl friend near one of the amps, and the Angel whose job it was to keep people away from the amps jerked him by the hair to pull him away. A fight broke out. The man tried to run away but several Angels rushed to join the fight. One pulled a knife and plunged it into the man's back, but he didn't fall. Instead, he turned, holding a gun. An Angel grabbed the gun, while another one stabbed him again and again. The man fell to his knees. Finally, 18-year-old Meredith Hunter lay dying in the sand.

All the while the Maysles brothers' cameras were rolling, capturing the horror of Meredith Hunters' murder in the film *Gimme Shelter.*

In the meantime, the Stones stopped playing, unaware of what was going on. A doctor made his way through the crowd and Meredith Hunter was carried off to die. A subdued Jagger—he still didn't know that a man has been stabbed to death at his feet—resumed singing. The Stones played several more songs, concluding with 'Street Fighting Man.'

Altamont was over. One man had been fatally stabbed, two more were killed in their sleeping bags by a hit-and-run driver, and another on a bad trip drowned when he jumped into a canal.

The tragedy of Altamont only served to reinforce the Stones' demonic presence. Public outcry was so great afterwards that the Stones dropped 'Sympathy for the Devil' from their act for six years.

After Altamont, the Stones returned to London for two more concerts and then began another period of inactivity, although Mick's personal life in an uproar. While the Stones were on tour in the States, Marianne Faithfull had left Mick for Mario Schifano, an italian painter and director. She later returned to Mick, but the relationship had disintegrated beyond repair and would soon end.

Marianne Faithfull disappeared from the public eye following her breakup with Jagger. In 1977, she again embarked on a recording career with the release of her first album in over 10 years.

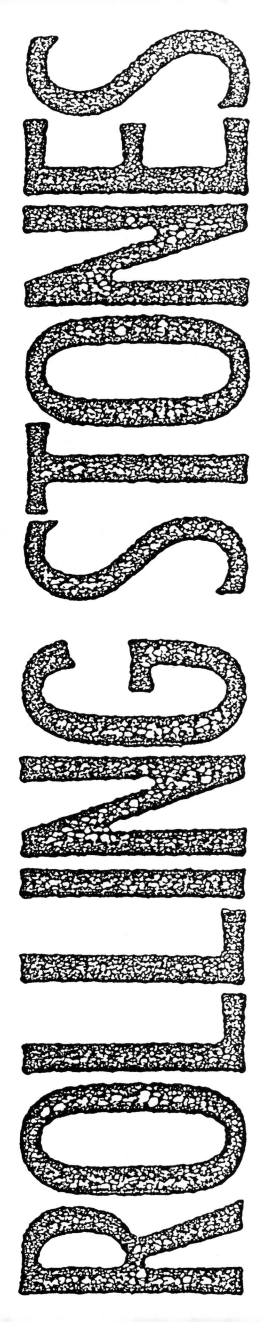

# THE WORLD'S GREATEST ROCK AND ROLL BAND

**A**s the tumultuous 1960s drew to a close, the Stones had begun calling themselves the world's greatest rock and roll band. With the breakup of the Beatles, the Rolling Stones—for the first time in their history—were the undisputed champions and there was no group that could even come close to challenging that claim.

In September 1970, the live album *Get Yer Ya-Ya's Out!* was released and quickly went gold, as did all the Stones' albums by this time. It had been recorded on 27 and 28 November 1969, during the tour that had climaxed at Altamont.

The new decade saw several changes for the Stones. By this time the Stones, with the exception of Charlie, were spending most of the year in their villas in the south of France to avoid taxes and drug arrests. Mick finally found the woman he wanted to marry— Nicaraguan fashion model Bianca Perez Morena de Macias. Mick met Bianca after the Stones' performance at L'Olympia in Paris during the tour of Europe in the fall of 1970. She soon joined Mick on tour, and when the tour was over she moved in with him at Stargroves.

The wedding of the decade took place on 13 May 1971 in St Tropez, with a guest list that read like a page out of Who's Who. Mick and Bianca quickly became favorites among the international jet-setters. Bianca merited 84 mentions in 'The Andy Warhol Diaries,' while Mick received 66. Mick's marriage was met with disdain by die-hard rock and rollers. Even Keith was dismayed by his good

*Sticky Fingers (below, left) was the first album released on the Stones' own label. The formation of their own label marked the beginning of a new era as the Stones took control of their financial situation, but the move into the world of business was not without its problems. Keith (page 65) would grow frustrated as Mick became more involved in business dealings, and their differences almost led to the dissolution of the band.*

*Exile on Main Street (below, right),a double album, is among their best.*

*Opposite page: Designed for the 1969 tour, this poster was never used.*

friend's marriage, and in a show of defiance, he sent an ashtray flying through a plate glass window. Mick and Bianca's daughter Jade was born on 21 October 1971.

Prior to the wedding, the Stones toured Britain in March of 1971, their first tour in almost five years. The loyal Stones' fans eagerly snatched up tickets, fearful of missing the chance to see the Stones before they ran off to their self-imposed exile in France.

Mick had always been a shrewd businessman, and now the Stones sought to improve their financial status. To that end, they formed their own company, Rolling Stones Records, a subsidiary of Atlantic. Marshall Chess, son of the founder of Chess Records, was made the president of the fledgling company.

## STICKY FINGERS

The first album released in 1971 under the new label—*Sticky Fingers*—featured the now famous lips and lapping tongue logo designed by legendary pop artist Andy Warhol. The zipper and jeans album cover was also the brainchild of Andy Warhol, who was hired by the Stones at an exorbitant fee to design the cover. (Warhol later designed the cover for *Love You Live*.)

Because it contained such songs as 'Brown Sugar' (a slang term for brown heroin), *Sticky Fingers* was labeled a heavy drug album. Other drug references could supposedly be found in 'Sister Morphine,' 'Dead Flowers' (heroin again) and 'Moonlight Mile' (cocaine, as in 'with a head full of snow.') 'Sister Morphine' was co-written by Marianne Faithfull, but she was never officially credited with the song.

'Brown Sugar' provoked controversy from another angle as well. The lyrics, although not easily heard, were also interpreted as sexist and racist. The words brown sugar were interpreted as a reference to the slave girls discussed in the song. As is characteristic of the Stones' style, Mick's voice is downplayed by mixing it into the

instrumental track. Early in his career Mick had learned to mumble the words in the fashion of blues singers.

The album also features 'Wild Horses,' which Keith claims has to do with his reluctance to leave his two-month-old son to tour the United States. Mick, however, had supposedly told Marianne Faithfull that the song was written for her. The other tracks include 'Bitch,' 'You Got To Move,' 'I Got the Blues,' 'Sway' and 'Can't You Hear Me Knocking.' The album stands today as one of their best.

## EXILE ON MAIN STREET

The Stones' next album—released in May 1972, a year after *Sticky Fingers*—would receive even higher praise, although at first *Exile on Main Street* was seen as a rambling sort of mess. Seemingly without any contrasts, it lacked an experimental edge. One has to listen hard to the album to understand and appreciate it. On one hand, *Exile on Main Street* gives a strong dose of hard-hitting rock and roll, as in 'Tumbling Dice' and 'Rip this Joint.' Other songs speak of death, despair and the dark side of life, as in 'Torn and Frayed,' a song that frankly addresses Keith's addiction. The influence of Gram Parsons, who had introduced Keith to the subtleties of honky-tonk music, is felt throughout the album. *Exile* fittingly closes with 'Soul Survivor,' a declaration that this band will survive.

The double album was recorded at Keith's villa Nellcote in the south of France between July and November of 1971. Following Mick's marriage to Bianca, Keith had turned his energies into creating a recording studio, thereby allowing him to stay at home and record. There was also the issue of Keith's addiction to heroin. Life was simpler if the band could to come to Keith. The chance of a drug bust was lessened and the band could work according to their schedule, not a studio's.

*With his marriage to Bianca (above), Mick became a jetsetter—much to the dismay of Keith.*

*Right: Mick takes the helm between concert performances in Hawaii, early in 1973. Opposite page: The Stones at the height of their success.* Sticky Fingers *had just been released—to much acclaim—and* Exile on Main Street *was soon to follow.*

## THE LAPPING TONGUE TOUR

Exile on Main Street was released a few weeks before the Stones' tour of the United States. Planning for the tour had begun months in advance. Tired of playing huge places like Madison Square Garden, the Stones wanted to concentrate on smaller houses, but the time required to please all their fans would drag the tour out for eight or nine months. In the end, financial considerations won out and the Stones played stadiums, flying from city to city in their private jet, The Lapping Tongue. Under the direction of tour manager Peter Rudge, the tour turned into a media event that would be observed and dutifully recorded by such illustrious writers as Truman Capote and Terry Southern.

The memory of Altamont lingered on, however, and security was heightened, with special attention being paid to Jagger. Two security guards were assigned to the Stones, and one was attached to Mick at all times when he wasn't in his hotel room.

On the night the tour opened in Vancouver about 2000 people tried to crash the concert. They broke down a corrugated metal

70

**At top:** *Keith Richards. In recent years, the British press, in counterpoint to Nancy Reagan's well-known anti-drug slogan, dubbed Keith 'The man who just said yes.'*

**Above:** *Behind the scenes of the Lapping Tongue Tour, with Mick and assorted members of the Stones Touring Party.* **Opposite page:** *Mick, after the tour.*

door before police were able to hold them off. Before the Stones appeared, several bottles thrown by the members of the audience shattered on the stage. During the second number, a fight broke out and an iron railing was ripped out of place and heaved toward the stage.

In Montreal, an explosive destroyed a truck holding amplifiers and other equipment. In Seattle, police confiscated a .22 caliber automatic pistol from one concert-goer and knives from several others. 'Sympathy for the Devil' had been dropped from the act, but 'Midnight Rambler' incited men to crawl on the stage, begging Mick to whip them with his belt.

In spite of these darker moments, the tour was essentially an endless party, with the members of the Stones rather sizable entourage dubbing themselves the Stones Touring Party, or STP for short. Tequila Sunrises were the drink of choice, and legend has it that the drink was *invented* on this tour. In Chicago, the Stones stayed with Hugh Hefner at the Playboy Mansion.

Even before the United States tour concluded, tour manager Peter Rudge began planning a tour of the Pacific, beginning in Hawaii and ending in Australia. Japan, where the Stones had never toured, was to be the centerpiece of the tour. Negotiations with Japan were running smoothly, with the band agreeing to donate 20 percent of their profits to charities selected by the Japanese. Contracts were signed and tickets sold, but suddenly Mick's visa was denied, based on his drug bust of 1969. Since other rock and roll stars with drug convictions behind them had been permitted to tour the country, it seemed that Japan was singling out Jagger. The end result is that everyone lost. The Japanese fans were denied the Stones, and the Stones were left in limbo from 22 January, the date of their last Hawaiian concert, and 11 February, the opening of the New Zealand leg of the tour. Their working permit for the United States expired 26 January, leaving them with time on their hands and no place to call home.

In the midst of the Japanese negotiations, the Stones did a benefit for the victims of the earthquake of 23 December 1972 that ravaged Managua. Cynics said the Stones did the show to win points with the Japanese. A simpler explanation could be found in Mick's Nicaraguan wife, Bianca. The two of them also flew to Managua with 2000 typhoid inoculations.

With their grand slam of albums—*Beggar's Banquet, Let It Bleed, Sticky Fingers* and *Exile on Main Street*—the Stones were unequivocally the world's greatest rock and roll band, but they were entering a time of transition—the effects of which would be seen in their music.

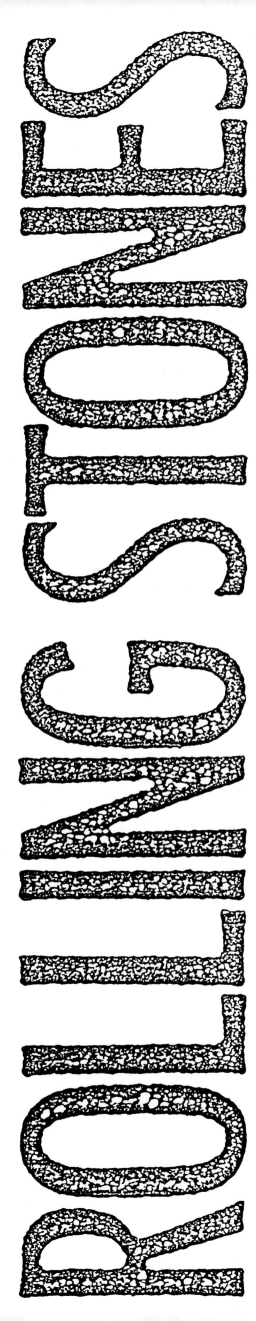

**ROLLING STONES**

# SLIPPING IN THE SEVENTIES

**G**oat's Head Soup, released in September 1973, failed to receive the praise that *Exile on Main Street* did, but it yielded the hits 'Angie' and 'Heartbreaker.' In retrospect, it represents the beginning of a period of decline for the Stones. Mick and Keith—using the pseudonym 'Glimmer Twins'—took complete control of production after *Goat's Head Soup,* but that didn't seem to help matters. Something was lost and Keith's addiction to heroin undoubtedly played a part in what was missing. 'Dancing with Mr D' seems a clear reference to Keith's problem, while 'Angie' is such a morose song that it must have been written under the influence of drugs.

Without some sort of controversy surrounding its debut, *Goat's Head Soup* would not have lived up to the public's expectations. Most radio stations refused to play the song 'Star Star' because it contained objectionable language.

Unlike the early years, when the Stones were on the road almost non-stop, in the 1970s a year—often more—would pass between concert tours. With a new album out the Stones toured Europe in September and October of 1973. Their return to Great Britain was greeted enthusiastically. Headlines announced the return of the Stones, and the four shows at Wembley Pool sold out the morning tickets went on sale. It had been two years since Britain's premiere rock and roll group had graced the island with its presence.

*A look at the 1975 Tour of the*

*Americas. Page 73: Mick, shirtless*

*and made-up. Above: Bill Wyman on*

*stage. Far right: With Mick Taylor's*

*resignation, the Stones were once*

*again searching for a new guitarist.*

*They found Ron Wood. Supposedly on*

*loan from the Faces, Woody soon*

*became a permanent fixture of the*

*Stones, adding a much needed dose*

*of enthusiasm. On stage as well as*

*off, Ron Wood and Keith (opposite*

*page, below) were a pair to be*

*reckoned with.*

# IT'S ONLY ROCK 'N' ROLL

The next year saw the release of *It's Only Rock 'n' Roll* (October 1974), which found hits in the Stones' cover of the Temptations' 'Ain't to Proud to Beg' and the title tune. Like *Goat's Head Soup* before it, the album lacked focus and punch.

*It's Only Rock 'n' Roll* was Mick Taylor's last album with the Rolling Stones. Technically, he may have been the best musician among the Stones, but he never fit in. Faced with the choice of succumbing to the decadent life style of the Stones or leaving the band, he chose the latter.

The Stones were once again looking for a new guitarist. Numerous session men auditioned and, in fact, appeared on *Black and Blue,* the Stones next album. By the time the Stones kicked off their 1975 American tour Ron Wood had joined their ranks. Wood was nominally committed to Rod Stewart and the Faces, and he was only going to 'help' the Stones with the tour, but all involved knew that Woody was now a Rolling Stone. (Although he played with both groups simultaneously, the Faces disbanded soon after Wood joined the Stones.) Ron Wood (born 1 June 1947) was no stranger to the Stones. He first heard the Stones at the Crawdaddy Club when he was a kid tagging along with his older brothers, who played with Alexis Korner (of Blues Incorporated) and Cyril Davis. It was said that Woody blew two chords out of three, but with his spiky hair he fit in well with the rest of the crew. What he did do was unite the band at a time when they were drifting apart. Together, he and Keith painstakingly worked out two-guitar parts, which expanded Charlie's part in rhythm-making. In time, Woody would also play a bigger part in songwriting, though most songs would continue to be by Jagger and Richards.

Before the 1975 tour could begin, the Stones had to deal with Keith and the immigration officials. If he could prove that there was not one speck of heroin in his blood he would be issued a working permit. This condition gave rise to the famous blood replacement

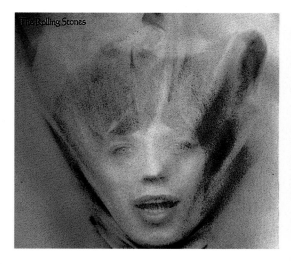

story. According to the tabloids, Keith went to a clinic in Switzerland and had all the blood in his body replaced with clean, fresh blood. However, medical authorities at the University of California Medical Center in San Francisco vehemently maintain that this procedure could never have been performed.

## THE TOUR OF THE AMERICAS, 1975

The announcement of the tour was made during an impromptu performance on the back of a truck rolling down Fifth Avenue in New York. If the last US tour had been a media event, this one was an extravaganza. The set used 150 tons of lights and the stage was a flower whose petals opened up to reveal the Stones. During 'Star Star' a gigantic rubber phallus popped up for Mick to punch and pummel.

Thanks in part to the addition of the energetic, high-spirited Ronnie Wood, the Stones were at their performing best. For years, Mick had been the unchallenged king of the stage. Now he would suddenly find himself upstaged as Woody made a mad dash at the audience. At other times Woody would sneak up behind Mick

and ham it up for the crowd or try to bait Bill Wyman out of his stoic's pose back in the corner. Woody was often so preoccupied with his on-stage antics that Keith had the dubious honor of making sure that Woody's playing stayed on track. Keyboardist Billy Preston and percussionist Ollie Brown were also on hand to lend their skills to the show.

The Stones returned 'Sympathy for the Devil' to their repertoire, and while the devil did remain in check, the tabloids preached against the Stones' 'demonic influence on our children' and castigated the Stones for flaunting 'the timeless values that have made us a great people.' If the Stones in particular were not the target of the tabloids' headlines, then rock and roll in general was. A church minister in Florida blamed the high rate of pregnancy among unmarried girls on rock music, citing the statistic that of the 1000 unwed mothers in his parish, 984 had become pregnant while listening to rock and roll.

Despite the screaming headlines, the 1975 tour was almost completely free from incident. As could almost be predicted, that rock and roll pirate, Keith Richards, was the source of trouble. In a drive from Memphis to Dallas, Keith was pulled over by a policeman in an unmarked car. He was cited with reckless driving and carrying a knife—a break for Keith since the officer mistook his cocaine for tooth powder.

The Stones reconvened in April 1976 for the European leg of the tour, where the glitz and glamour were even more heightened. The Stones hadn't played London in three years and one million requests for tickets were made by mail. Only a tenth of the demand could be filled, even though the Stones doubled their three-concert series at Earls Court Arena. Prior to the concert, Jagger personally toured the arena to check on the seats and facilities. After rehearsals, he stopped his car and handed out free tickets to kids on the street. At Jagger's request, free refreshments were served to people waiting in line at the box office.

To some critics, however, the Stones were all glamour and no substance. Stage theatrics had replaced the substance and energy of their music and came up lacking. In concert, the Stones played only a few tracks from their latest album *Black and Blue* (April 1976), which was released just as the European tour began. According to the concert review in *The Times,* the audience 'accepted rather than seized on' the songs, as they waited for the Stones to delve into their collection of hits from the past.

## BLACK AND BLUE

The album followed the usual formula for the Stones—it sold well and generated controversy with its poster of a woman in bondage. Though *Black and Blue* was snapped up in the stores, many fans were disappointed with the album and its explorations into

**Far left: *Ollie Brown joined the***

***Stones for their 1975 tour.* Left:**

***Charlie Watts in action.***

**Above: *The gigantic rubber phallus***

***provided a stunning visual effect—***

***one that was guaranteed to delight***

***the audience while enraging parents***

***and the popular press.***

*Below: Billy Preston was also part of the theatrical 1975 tour. Emerging from the group, Preston took center stage for two numbers and almost made the crowd forget about the Stones.*

*Opposite page: Even with guest performers and mammoth props, Mick still managed to be the focus of attention.*

disco, reggae and salsa. The number of studio musicians used in its creation also added to the album's unevenness. *Black and Blue* was not a total loss—the single 'Fool To Cry' did fairly well. *Black and Blue* also features Billy Preston on keyboards for 'Melody.' In general, however, the album was a far cry from the Stones' brilliant earlier work, and many longtime fans were ready to give up on them; others just shrugged their shoulders and hoped that the next album would be better.

The three albums produced in the wake of *Exile on Main Street* showed the Stones at their worst, the result of boredom and lack of interest.

Tensions were running high and the tolerance that the Stones had once had for each other was on the wane. As Mick became more a part of high society, Keith seemed more determined to play the part of the outlaw and continued to trash hotel rooms, crash cars, and carry guns and knives. Keith grew less tolerant of the theatrics that Mick had allowed on the 1975 tour, and Mick became equally impatient with Keith's arrest record. In the past, the Stones were always able to overcome adversity, but some of their fans began to wonder if they would survive the upheaval created by Mick and Keith's differences.

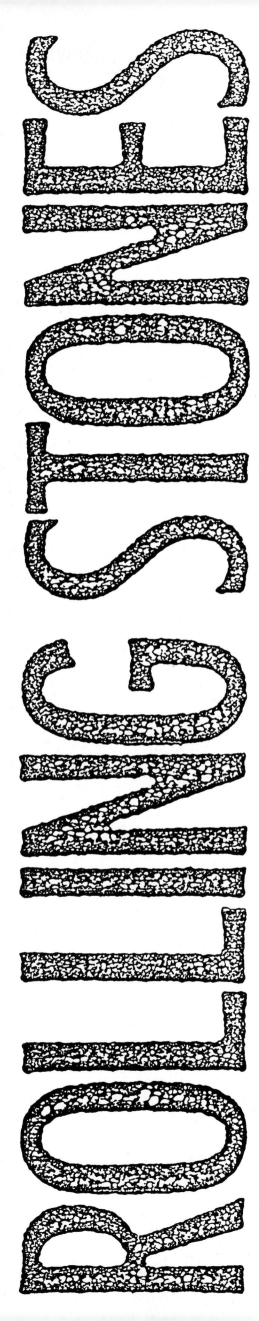

ROLLING STONES

# HARD TIMES FOR THE GLIMMER TWINS

**A**s 1977 began, the Stones seemed to be back on track. Rejuvenated on stage by Ron Wood, they decided to do another live album. Rather than do a condensed version of another stadium tour, the Stones were determined to work in performances at small clubs and scheduled a recording stop at the El Mocambo nightclub in Toronto.

Despite their well-laid plans, the trip to Toronto came close to sounding the death knell for the Stones. The Stones, all except Keith, arrived in Toronto on 20 February 1977 to rehearse at El Mocambo. After repeated transatlantic calls and an angry telegram, Keith showed up five days late. A search by customs officials of Anita's 28 pieces of luggage revealed a piece of hashish and a blackened spoon. Anita was held for questioning and released pending analysis of the spoon. Three days later the Royal Canadian Mounted Police charged into Keith and Anita's suite with a warrant for her arrest. In the room they discovered an ounce of pure heroin—enough to bust Keith for trafficking. If convicted, the charge could lead to a sentence of seven years to life. The arrest led to yet another rift between Keith and Mick, fueling speculation that this really was the end of the Rolling Stones.

Amid the predictions of their imminent demise, the Stones taped their performances at El Mocambo, with the sessions producing some of their finest blues since the days at the Crawdaddy Club. It was a return to their roots—to the music of Muddy Waters and Chuck Berry. Their performance was electrifying, the crowd

was awed and amazed. One Canadian journalist described the Stones as the best bar band he had ever seen. The music from El Mocambo produced the brightest spot on *Love You Live,* the Stones' third live album. The rest of the album was recorded in Paris during the Stones' 1976 tour and featured classic Stones songs, from 'Get Off Of My Cloud' to 'Sympathy for the Devil.'

In the audience at El Mocambo was Margaret Trudeau, wife of the Canadian prime minister. A few days later she left for New York—and so did most of the Stones—causing the papers to speculate that she had run off to be with Mick Jagger.

While the other Stones were in New York, Keith, under bail, was forced to stay in Canada. Keith eventually received permission to leave Canada 'to practice his profession' until his trial in October. He also was granted a special visa to enter the United States and undergo treatment for heroin addiction at the Stevens Psychiatric Center in New York.

Keith's trial was held in October of 1978. Plea bargaining reduced the charge from trafficking to possession. Much to everyone's surprise, Keith was placed on a year's probation and given a suspended sentence. He was ordered to continue treatment for heroin addiction, with an additional stipulation that he perform a benefit concert for the blind.

On 14 April 1979 Keith Richards—with the assistance of Mick Jagger, Ron Wood and the New Barbarians—performed the first of two benefits for the blind in fulfillment of his sentence for possession of heroin.

The Stones had once again overcome what seemed to be an insurmountable hurdle. Mick and Keith had patched up their differences. Keith's victory in court came as a welcome surprise, and even more significantly, he was on his way to winning his personal battle with heroin. The end of his drug addiction signaled the end of his dozen years with Anita, a painful but necessary break.

## SOME GIRLS

While waiting for his trial, Keith and the rest of the Stones started work on the album that would be *Some Girls.* Featuring the hits 'Miss You' and 'Shattered,' *Some Girls* was the Stones' biggest selling album to date. Critics maligned 'Miss You,' saying that the Stones had sold out to disco. In the song's defense, Mick pointed out that 'Miss You' had been written long before the movie *Saturday Night Fever* ushered in the disco craze. Compared to the dismal output of the previous years, *Some Girls* (June 1978) was the best music the Stones had done in years, with some people declaring that it was

Page 81: *Keith and Mick, aka the Glimmer Twins. In spite of their smiling face, the two were headed for hard times. In February 1977, Keith (opposite page) was charged with trafficking heroin, meanwhile Mick (above) grew tired of Keith's constant run-ins with the law.*

84

their best album since *Let It Bleed*. Mick commented that *Some Girls* had continuity without the holes. Keith attributed the album's success to the tightness of the band; *Some Girls* was Ron Wood's first complete album as a Stone, so there were no other musicians working on it. As Keith put it, 'We've been away for a bit and came back with a bang.' A significant factor in the album's success was that Keith was finally off heroin.

The album shows the Stones having fun making music. In 'Far Away Eyes' Mick takes on the persona of a redneck. In 'Respectable' he pokes fun at society (and perhaps too at Bianca, his soon to be ex-wife). *Some Girls* was released at the time when punk rockers were challenging anything old, particularly the dinosaur bands. 'Respectable' showed the Stones were no dinosaurs; they hadn't lost their attitude of flippant defiance. Keith's impending trial inspired a song as well: 'After all is said and done/I did all right and had my fun/But I will walk before they make me run.'

The lyrics of the title track provoked another public outcry. The Reverend Jesse Jackson, head of Operation PUSH (People United to Save Humanity) even called for the record to be banned, calling the lyrics sexist and racist. Jackson met with Ahmet Ertegun, chairman of the board of Atlantic Records (which distributes the Stones' albums in the United States) and threatened pickets and boycotts unless some sort of resolution was reached. Given that black urban blues provided the inspiration for the Stones' music, the public's reaction was ironic if not way out of proportion. The Stones refused to censor the record, but Earl McGrath, president of Rolling Stones Records, did issue the following statement on the band's behalf:

'It never occurred to us that our parody of certain stereotypical attitudes would be taken seriously by anyone who heard the entire lyrics of the song in question. No insult was intended, and if any was taken, we sincerely apologize.'

By the time that *Some Girls* was released, Mick and Bianca's

*In 1978, the acrimonious marriage between Mick and Bianca (above) came to an end. Since then Mick has been involved with model Jerry Hall (opposite page). They have two children and a seemingly stable relationship, but after one battle in divorce court, Mick has no plans for remarriage.*

**Love You Live (right) captured the magic at the El Mocambo nightclub in Toronto, while Some Girls (far right) represented their best album in years.**

marriage was unofficially over. Bianca, who is reputed to have said 'My marriage ended on my wedding day,' retained Marvin Mitchelson, of palimomy fame, to handle her divorce from Mick. She filed in California to take advantage of the state's community property laws, which grant a wife half of her husband's assets.

In the meantime, Mick had been seeing Jerry Hall, an American model. Blonde and unpretentious, Jerry represented the antithesis of Bianca. A former distinguished Dairy Queen employee in Mesquite, Texas, she had been a wild party girl in Paris and posed in only high heels and riding crop for photographer Helmut Newton.

# THE NINTH NORTH AMERICAN TOUR

On 10 June 1978 the Stones launched their Ninth North American Tour in Lakeland, Florida. They played large stadiums, such as the Superdome, but also managed to work in a few nights at smaller clubs. At their first appearance at New York's Palladium since their 1964 tour, the Stones performed before a crowd of 3000. *Melody Maker* called the show 'their best since Richmond in 1963.'

By the time the tour, which made $9 million, concluded in Oakland, California, 760,000 people in 25 cities had seen the Stones play.

Although their fans didn't know it at the time, the Stones were entering a cycle of limited touring, in which they toured only every three years.

# EMOTIONAL RESCUE

*Emotional Rescue* (June 1980) continued in the same vein as *Some Girls.* Though not quite up to the level of *Some Girls,* the album shows the Stones exploring new ground. With *Emotional Rescue,* they are experimenting, moving into new directions, albeit sometimes more successfully than others. The title track, for

example, has what Charlie Watts calls a 'half-reggae' rhythm. The song features Mick on piano singing in a falsetto voice. 'Send It To Me' shows the Stones perfecting the rhythm of reggae. The Stones returned to their blues roots with 'Down in the Hole,' the B side of 'Emotional Rescue.' The second single off the album was 'She's So Cold,' a tongue-in-cheek look at Mick's love life. In 'All About You,' Keith Richards chronicles the end of his longtime love affair with Anita Pallenberg. 'Where the Boys Go' and 'Let Me Go' were more in the traditional Stones style and must have been a relief for those fans who feared the Stones were moving off in too many wrong directions.

The Stones didn't tour with *Emotional Rescue,* although at the time Mick talked about touring Europe and Australia. There was even talk of a tour in China. But it was only talk.

On 12 March 1981 the Stones released *Sucking in the Seventies,* an off-the-wall collection of greatest hits recorded during the pre-

*Keith's trial was scheduled for October 1978, but his lawyers were able to secure permission for him to leave Canada for the 1978 tour. The Ninth North American Tour, which ran from June 10 to July 26, once again prompted speculation that this would be the Stones' last tour. Clockwise, from above: Mick Jagger, Keith Richards and Charlie Watts.*

ceding decade. Tracks included a live version of 'When the Whip Comes Down' and 'Everything's Turning to Gold.'

## TATTOO YOU

*Tattoo You* (August 1981), which outsold *Some Girls,* was regarded by many critics as the Stones' best effort since *Exile on Main Street.* The album delivers the promise begun with *Some Girls.* Like that album, it shows the Stones ready for the 1980s.

Back in 1962, none of the Stones would have imagined that almost 20 years later they would still be together. By time the 1980s arrived the Stones had attained mythic proportions. Although the albums in the mid-1970s provide irrefutable evidence that the band had gone slack, their concert performances—rare though they were—proved that there was still nothing else like them in rock and roll. With *Tattoo You,* the Stones again sounded like the great rock and roll band that they are. The album, with the number two hit, 'Start Me Up,' was their biggest seller yet. On the charts for 22

**Above:** *Keith may have kicked heroin, but cigarettes and bourbon still rank among his vices.*

**Opposite page:** *Proving that he still has what it takes, Mick Jagger ignites the crowd on the 1978 tour.*

weeks, 'Start Me Up' was a throw-away track that had been on the shelf for the last few years. The second single from *Tattoo You,* 'Waiting on a Friend' is a tribute to the twenty-year friendship between Mick and Keith. A video accompanying the single featured the two of them walking through New York City. 'Neighbors' is another song inspired by Keith. Mick wrote it about all those people who have lived near Keith and had to endure his stereo blaring at all times of the night.

Other tracks include 'Black Limousine' (co-written by Ron Wood) and 'Little T & A,' featuring Keith on lead vocals, and 'Heaven.' 'Heaven' is an unusual number for the Stones, in both style and production. The original track was laid down with just Mick and Charlie.

*Tattoo You* differed from the Stones' previous albums in that Charlie Watts comes through clearer on it than he had in their past albums, thanks to the mixing of Bob Clearmountain. The album also features jazz great Sonny Rollins on tenor saxophone on 'Waiting on a Friend' and 'Slave.'

While the album was climbing the charts, rumors of trouble in paradise abounded. The album was reportedly produced amidst feuds between Keith and Mick over how a song should be done. Working together they arrived at the basic tracks, but then each one would independently devise a mix and there the trouble started. The press had them erasing each other's mixes. The situation never got quite as bad as that, but there were some heated debates over which version was better.

Citing Bill Wyman's solo endeavors as evidence of his imminent departure, the press persisted in reporting that Bill was leaving the band. In addition to his solo albums—*Stone Alone* (1976) and *Monkey Grip* (1974)—Bill did production work on two blues and jazz records and a book of photographs about Marc Chagall. Though it wasn't released in the States, Bill's single 'Je Suis Un Rock Star' topped the charts in Britain and Europe in 1981. Bill was never in the limelight like Mick or Keith so it easy for the public to label him as detached from the group. To the unknowing eye, detachment is just one step away from disillusionment.

## THE 1981 UNITED STATES TOUR

Rumors of all sizes and shapes were finally put to bed as the Stones embarked on another tour of the United States, their first since the 1978 tour three years earlier. By this time the Stones were older than many of their fans. High school students mingled with fans from the 1960s, some of whom were still hippies, others lawyers and accountants. Although Mick Jagger at one time allegedly said that he did want to singing 'Satisfaction' when he was 30 (or 32 or 35, depending on the source and his age at the time) here he was at 38, with no sign of stopping. To show their younger fans just why they are the world's greatest rock and roll band, the Stones incorporated a number of older, lesser known songs in the repertoire. They opened the show with 'Under My Thumb' from the 1966 *Aftermath* album.

The tour opened on 25 September 1981 in Philadelphia at John F Kennedy Stadium before 90,000 fans. From the opening strains of 'Under My Thumb,' the Stones grabbed the audience and never let them go for more than two hours. Wearing a scarlet T-shirt, white wool leotards and a yellow quilted jacket, Mick Jagger pranced across the stage in his inimitable style. Keith Richards crouched low, combat style, while Ron Wood provided the trademark licks for 'Let's Spend the Night Together,' 'Let It Bleed,' 'All Down the Line' and 'Honky Tonk Women.' As always, Wyman and Watts provided the steady rhythm and blues bass line. The Stones were reportedly dissatisfied with their first performance and ironed out a few bugs before they set out across the country, dropping a few numbers that didn't work on outdoor stages.

The stage, designed by Japanese artist Kazuhide Yamakazi, was the largest mobile set ever built: 64 feet wide with 80-foot ramps stretching out from the sides. Strips of silk 150 feet long fluttered into the audience. The gigantic scrims surrounding the stage supposedly contained enough cloth to outfit the sails of three clipper ships. In Buffalo, high winds destroyed the set and a duplicate had to be constructed. The winds kept knocking the microphone into Jagger's teeth, necessitating dental work to repair the loosened diamond that he had embedded in his incisor in 1975.

The tour was the smoothest, most professional of their career, however. Bill Graham, who replaced Peter Rudge as tour manager, kept the show running like a well-oiled machine. Touring was now big business, complete with a corporate sponsor—Jovan, the perfume empire. Even the once simple task of buying and selling tickets took on momentous proportions. An independent auditing firm was hired to handle the distribution of tickets in the New York City area. Using a process similar to that used by *Time* and American Express for direct mailings, the auditors determined the potential number of Stones' fans in each Zip (Postal) Code area and allocated the tickets accordingly. More than four million pieces of mail were received in the 56 hours following the announcement of the concert, forcing the Post Office to hire 125 part-time employees to handle the onslaught of mail.

*After a lull of three years, the Stones went on tour again. Opposite page, above: Mick struts his stuff. Opposite page, below: Bill Wyman, the archetypal stoical British bass player. Wyman is also an amateur photographer and the band's historian.*

*At top: Mick shares center stage with Ron Wood, and (above) with Keith Richards.*

Although a 16-year-old girl was killed following a fall from a 50-foot ramp, the concerts were not punctuated by the riots that marked the shows of the 1960s. The tragedy of Altamont was a distant memory and, in truth, was ancient history to those fans who were mere toddlers in 1969.

Offstage, the Stones created a flurry of activity in hotel lobbies as fans tried to steal a glimpse of their idols, and the hotels were willing to let the Stones stay in the nice rooms this time because they didn't trash the rooms the last time around. It would seem that the bad boys of rock had grown up. Once considered the scourge of society, now the Stones provided tidbits for the gossip columnists. In every big city, clubs were packed with fans hoping for a surprise appearance by the Stones.

The tour was the largest grossing tour thus far in the history of rock and roll, netting in excess of $40 million. (Their 1989 tour would command an even greater amount.) When all was said and done, the Stones proved once again that they were the greatest rock and roll band in the world. From the moment the show started Jagger never stopped moving. Whirling about the stage, bathed in lights, he was the focus of the performance. Wyman, Watts and Woods were pieces in a powerful rock and roll machine, but what held it all together was Keith Richards, the heart and soul of the Roll-

*Though Mick (opposite page, above) may have stolen more of the spotlight, Keith Richards (right) provided the glue that held the Rolling Stones together during their 1981 tour.*

*Above: Ron Wood. He and Keith taught Mick to play the guitar (opposite page, below).*

ing Stones. His guitar urged the others on, forcing them to respond to the rhythms he was bouncing off them.

As soon as the tour was completed the Stones got down to the business of recording it for posterity. On 1 June 1982 the Stones released the single 'Going to A Go-Go' and the live album *Still Life*, which featured 10 cuts recorded throughout the tour. Eagerly snatched up by fans, old and young alike, *Still Life* reached number five and went gold. The single peaked at number 25. The documentary of the tour, Hal Ashby's *Let's Spend the Night Together* (released in early 1983) did only moderately well because it focused almost entirely on Jagger's stage work, didn't show the other band members but occasionally and had no documentary off-stage material like *Gimme Shelter* did.

The Stones were at the height of their commercial success. As performers, they were unequalled in the world of rock and roll. But the conflicts between Mick and Keith would keep them off the road until 1989.

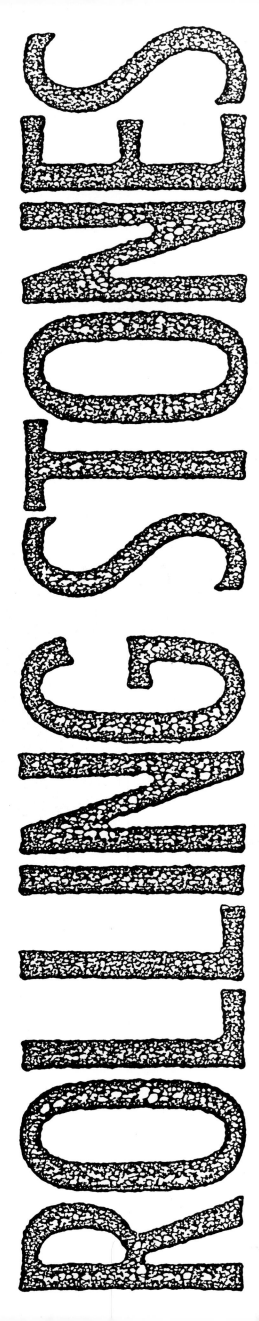

# INTO THE EIGHTIES

**A**fter completing their European tour, the Stones took a few months off, before starting work on their next album in October 1982 at the EMI studios in Paris. Sessions continued into November, but the album remained unfinished. After a six-month hiatus, the Stones reconvened, this time in Nassau, to finish the album—*Undercover.*

The first single from the album, 'Undercover of the Night,' was finally released on 1 November 1983, along with an elaborate video. The video depicted a kidnapping (of Jagger) in South America and the ensuing rescue (Jagger again as a different character). The single reached number nine and the album, *Undercover,* went to number four. The album also featured the hit 'She Was Hot.' Though *Undercover* sold over a million copies, it was the first time since 1969 that a new studio release album by the Stones failed to hit the number one spot. The Stones didn't tour with *Undercover,* but with their recent pattern of tours every three years that was not unusual.

## STONES ALONE

After *Undercover* was completed, Keith Richards took time off in 1983 to marry American model Patti Hansen. Meanwhile, Mick and Jerry Hall were awaiting the birth of their first child.

Mick also found the time to negotiate a multi-million dollar contract for the Stones with Columbia Records. In July 1984 the Stones

96

released *Rewind (1971-1984)*, probably to fill a contractual obligation for a greatest hits album. Only reaching number 86 on the charts, the album was followed a year later by an hour-long video that featured Mick Jagger and Bill Wyman strolling through a dusty store room, looking at video clips.

In the meantime, Jagger had been hard at work on his first solo album. Late in 1984 he traveled to Brazil with Julien Temple to shoot a series of videos for the album. 'Just Another Night,' Jagger's first solo single, was released on 23 January 1985. It peaked at number 12. The album *She's the Boss* reached number 13 in the United States and went platinum.

Rumors circulated that the Stones would tour the United States in the summer of 1985. A tour never happened, although members of the Stones did participate in the July 1985 Live Aid concerts to fight world hunger. Two nights before the concert Keith Richards and Ron Wood jammed with guitarist Lonnie Mack at New York's Star Cafe. Jagger watched from the balcony. At Live Aid, Richards and Wood appeared with Bob Dylan, but Mick teamed up with Tina Turner.

**Page 94:** *In the early 1980s, the Glimmer Twins went their separate ways. Seen here is a publicity shot of Mick, the solo artist.* She's the Boss *(above) was Jagger's first solo album. Meanwhile, Keith Richards married model Patti Hansen (right).*

**Opposite page:** *In July 1985 Ron Wood, Keith Richards and Mick Jagger performed at the Live Aid Concert, but not together. Jagger teamed up with Tina Turner, while Richards and Wood joined Bob Dylan.*

# DIRTY WORK

In spite of the differences between Keith and Mick, the Stones were back in Paris, working on another album, *Dirty Work.* As the album was nearing completion, longtime friend and cohort Ian Stewart died of a heart attack. Stu's death 'was the final nail in the coffin,' Keith later remarked. 'We all felt the glue had come undone.' The Stones dedicated the album to Stu.

*Dirty Work* (March 1986) is solid but not spectacular Stones. The first group effort produced under the mega-bucks contract with CBS Records, the album at times has a dullness that comes from rushing to meet a deadline. *Dirty Work* sold a million copies and peaked at number four, with the singles 'Harlem Shuffle' (number five) and 'One Hit (To the Body)' (number 28) also finding success. But perhaps the album is best remembered for its acrimonious production, with Mick and Keith constantly feuding. In the interviews that marked the album's release all the Stones alluded to the disagreements between Keith and Mick, and all of them—with the exception of Mick—were quoted as expecting a tour. No tour occurred.

In the absence of a tour, the Stones again went their separate ways. Charlie indulged his love of jazz and formed the Charlie Watts Orchestra, a big band ensemble whose tour of the United States in 1986 yielded a live album. Ron Wood couldn't stay away

*The rest of the Stones were not idle while Keith and Mick were squabbling. Above: Bill Wyman, the group historian, opened Sticky Fingers, a restaurant filled with items from his personal collection of Stones memorabilia. Right: Among other activities, Ron Wood wrote a book.*

*Opposite page: Keith Richards organized a concert in honor of Chuck Berry's sixtieth birthday. The Stones, and Keith especially, had been inspired by Berry since they were teenagers.*

from the road and showed up on tour with Bob Dylan and Tom Petty and the Heartbreakers. He also toured with Bo Diddley, and for a time managed a nightclub in Florida—Woody's on the Beach. Bill Wyman also forayed into the club world with a restaurant called Sticky Fingers. Molded in the Hard Rock Cafe tradition, the restaurant is decorated with Stones memorabilia. Mick Jagger recorded the title track for the soundtrack to the movie *Ruthless People.* The song made it only to Number 51. Keith Richards helped Aretha Franklin with a cover version of 'Jumpin' Jack Flash,' for the movie of the same name. In addition, Keith began organizing a sixtieth birthday concert for archetypal rock and roller Chuck Berry. Footage from the concert was featured in Taylor Hackford's film about Chuck Berry, *Hail! Hail! Rock 'n' Roll.*

It began to seem that the Rolling Stones were no more. Keith and Mick's bickering continued even when they were apart. 'Shoot Off Your Mouth' from *Primitive Cool,* Mick's second solo album, was a veiled barb at Keith. In turn, Keith's first solo album *Talk Is Cheap*

included 'You Don't Move Me'—his response to Jagger. Neither one's solo albums did very well. Mick's dance tunes, while slick, lacked the intensity of the his collaborations with Keith, and Keith's scratchy voice starts to wear over the course of an entire album. It would seem that the Glimmer Twins needed each other.

Though they call themselves twins, they are closer to alter egos. Keith was always the rock and roll purist, the musical conscience who would spend hours in the studio perfecting just one riff. Mick, on the other hand, was the rock and roller who never forgot his training at the London School of Economics. They fought about the future and the past, their own as well as the Rolling Stones. Through the years they argued about Mick becoming one of the beautiful people, about Keith refusing to leave his renegade years behind. They clashed over the direction the Rolling Stones should take, with Mick asserting they were moving forward with their explorations into 'current' music and Keith dissenting, believing they were selling out. For a time, their differences ruled. Finally, Jagger, having discovered 'There's no where else to go,' initiated the peace talks.

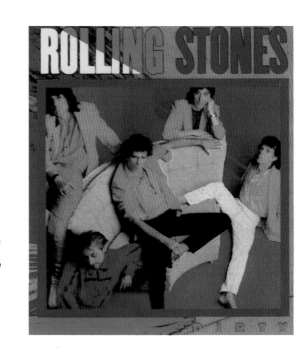

**Far left:** *Mick at Live Aid, July 1985, and (left, below) Keith with Bob Dylan. Though the rift between the two seemed to foretell the end of the Stones, Mick and Keith couldn't stay apart, and the Stones got together for a new album,* Dirty Work *(above).*

**Left, above:** *Mick and longtime companion Jerry Hall.*

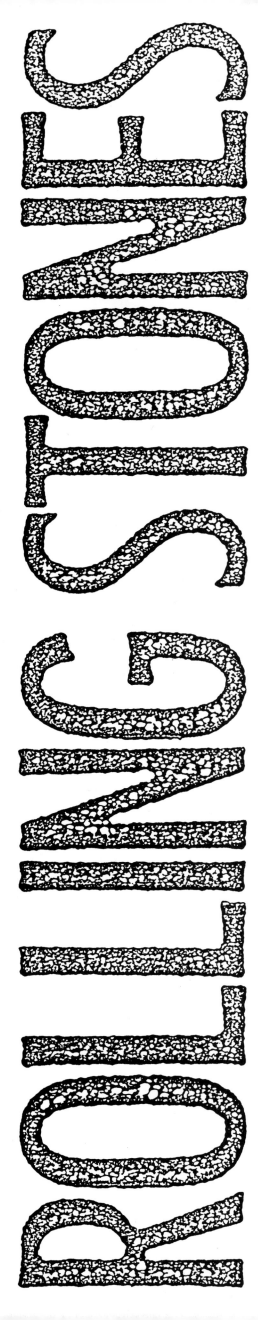

# STEEL WHEELS

n January 1988, Jagger and Richards met in Barbados to see if they could arrive at a truce. Their meeting set up the basis for the 1989 tour of North America as well as the beginning of a new album. With only a couple of chairs, a tape recorder and a few guitars, the pair rediscovered the magic that had made their songwriting work in the past. Keith contributed a few ideas that he hadn't used on his solo album, and within a few days, five or six songs were in the works. By the time they were finished they had the 12 tracks for *Steel Wheels* as well as an additional 40-odd songs, riffs and lyric ideas that ended up on the cutting room floor.

The next step was convincing the rest of the Stones that they were serious about making a new album. After getting caught in the cross fire of the Jagger-Richards feud during the making of the last album, Wood, Watts and Wyman were understandably reluctant to get involved in what could easily turn into another blow-up. Once all the Stones were assembled at the AIR Studio in Montserrat, it took only five weeks to record the basic tracks. The writing, recording and mixing took only six months, in contrast to previous albums, which often took a year or more to complete.

*Steel Wheels* (August 1989) is the Stones' best in a decade, made in the tradition of their great albums of the late 1960s and early 1970s. The first track 'Sad, Sad, Sad' opens with the characteristic hard-driving riffs of 'All Down the Line' or 'Bitch.' 'Mixed Emotions,' the first single from the album, is a pulverizing rocker, carrying more than a suggestion of the Jagger-Richards feud.

*Page 103: Together again—the Rolling Stones in 1989. And on the road, with Keith and his wife Patti (below) during the Steel Wheels Tour.*

*Opposite page: Mick Jagger takes command of the stage, demonstrating how powerful his voice remains.*

To the Stones, the album represents unification, a unification that goes deeper than getting back together. For one track, Keith and Mick returned to Morocco and the Master Musicians of Jajouka, whose music so captivated Brian Jones 20 years ago. The drums and pipes of the Master Musicians are featured on 'Continental Drift,' the most unusual track on the album.

In the midst of recording the album, Bill Wyman (who was 52 at the time) slipped away to wed 19-year-old Mandy Smith. In spite of Mandy's tender age, this was no whirlwind courtship—the two began dating when she was 13.

While working on the album, the Stones were busy planning a tour of North America. After a year of negotiations, the Stones selected Michael Cohl of Concert Productions International to manage the tour. With Cohl agreeing to take on all financial risks, profits to the Stones were estimated at $70 million, a figure that prompted people to wonder if the Stones had decided to tour again for the money. Of course they did and they were the first to admit it. Jagger, a shrewd businessman, understood that people have to receive a good return on their investment. Outrageous prices for tickets are acceptable, as long as the audience gets its money's worth.

And the Stones gave the audience their money's worth. As the lights went down to the sound of drums from 'Continental Drift,' a wall of flame roared across the stage. The crowd gasped as one, and suddenly the Rolling Stones burst into 'Start Me Up.' Throughout the entire two and a half hour concert, as they worked their way through their 25-year collection of hits, the Stones kept the crowd on their feet. The crowd responded equally to such Stones classics as 'Paint It, Black' and 'Gimme Shelter' as they did to songs from *Steel Wheels,* which Jagger politely asked to perform—'I hope you don't mind if we do a few songs from our new album.' He then teasingly reassured the crowd that they didn't need to worry about being conservative if they still liked the older material.

As is usual for a Stones concert, the biggest crowd pleaser is 'Satisfaction,' which they saved until the end of the show. The song over, the Stones departed amid thunderous applause, leaving the empty stage bathed in dim blue light. Then fireworks ripped across the stage, as the Stones burst into an encore of 'Jumpin' Jack Flash.'

The 1989 tour proved once again that the Rolling Stones are the world's greatest rock and roll band. Though their on-stage presence was considerably more subdued than that of the energetic Jagger, the rhythm section of Watts and Wyman never faltered. Ron Wood hopped about the stage, happy just to play the guitar while trading the occasional riff with Keith Richards. Richards took

**At top: *Stone-faced Bill Wyman***
***maintains a serious demeanor***
***throughout a concert. Above: Ron***
***Wood, in one of his more subdued***
***moods.***

**Opposite page: *Though 20 years***
***ago they never would have believed***
***it themselves, the Stones have shown***
***you're never too old to rock and roll.***

center stage for 'Before They Make Me Run' and 'Happy,' but most of the time was laid back, secure in his position as one of the best rock and roll guitarists.

Jagger, of course, was the perfect showman. He clearly knew every inch of the stage, dashing from one end to the other, never ignoring the crowds seated off to the side. From the opening number he mesmerized the audience, once and for all refuting the critics' complaint that he had become a parody of himself. An absolutely dynamic performer, his energy was boundless. He never let up (with the exception of the few songs on which Keith did lead vocals). Mick established an immediate rapport with the audience and kept up a cheerful, teasing banter throughout the concert. When the band played the Oakland Coliseum, he commended the crowd for their 'very incredible spirit' in the wake of the recent earthquake, never mentioning that the Stones had donated $500,000 to the Red Cross for relief efforts after the San Francisco earthquake and Hurricane Hugo in South Carolina. It's hard to believe that this is the same band that was once accused of being devil worshippers.

The Stones have mastered the art of playing in a stadium, a seemingly impossible task. The lighting, the set, the music—all worked together to transport a rock concert into the realm of theatre. With its scaffolding and tubes, the set of the *Steel Wheels* tour—which was designed to evoke the image of a city on the edge of decay, a city of abandoned oil refineries and crumbling factories—bore a striking resemblance to the Pompidou Center in Paris. Eight stories high and wider than a football field, the futuristic set was derelict and sinister, but its mood changed from hard to soft, from the dramatic to the comical. With the opening riffs of 'Honky Tonk Women,' two giant—at least 100 feet tall—inflatable dolls popped out of boxes on each side of the stage and swayed along with the music. The audience responded with cheers.

Stadium tours are not complete without a video screen, and the screen not only gave the people in the distant reaches of the stadium a view of what was happening on stage, the videos complemented the songs as well. At one point, the screen alternated images of the Stones early in their career with views of the stage. During '2000 Light Years From Home' the video transported the crowd back to the 'sixties' with brightly colored psychedelic images. As the song ended, psychedelic music continued to play as smoke engulfed the stage and the Stones disappeared from view for a few moments, letting the suspense build. When the smoke cleared, the band ripped into 'Sympathy for the Devil' with Jagger, dressed in a bright crimson jacket, high atop the set.

Tickets for the concerts, which averaged $28.50 (plus $4.50 fees), were snatched up within hours after they went on sale. The drawing power of the Stones was dramatically illustrated by their ability to sell out Shea Stadium for a week. As is usual for a show of this magnitude, fans waited overnight, camped out in sleeping bags, for tickets to go on sale. This time their ranks were joined by 40-year-old business executives in suits and ties who surreptitiously left work in order to stand in line. The intervening 20 years since *Let It Bleed* had seen quite a change in their appearance.

As with the Stones' previous tour, the audience was an eclectic mix. Middle-aged moms and dads from the suburbs, along with their children, were seated next to purple-haired punk rockers

decked out from head to toe in black leather. But the backbone of the Stones' following remains the fans who grew up listening to their music. The audience had more than its fair share of gray hair and age lines, but if people were concerned about growing old, it never showed, and in fact old age was the running joke of the evening. To introduce 'Ruby Tuesday,' Jagger mocked himself as well as the audience: 'We're going to slow things down now for the older members of the band as well as for you older hippies.'

When the Stones last went on last tour in 1981, the papers were filled with articles discussing their age and whether they had the stamina needed for rock and roll. In 1989 the question was even more pressing, for the Stones were not the only aging rock and rollers on the road again. In the summer of 1989—the twentieth anniversary of Woodstock—The Who, Jefferson Airplane and Bob Dylan all announced plans to tour. The people who once felt no one over thirty could be trusted were now well into middle age and still able to rock and roll.

Skeptics questioned the ability of a bunch of guys in their forties and fifties (Wyman, who turned 53 during the tour, is the oldest) to perform hard driving rock and roll. The skeptics' doubts were laid to rest in short order. The Stones took every city by storm, where it was *the* major event, the Super Bowl of rock and roll. As the Stones proved in 1981 and again in 1989, age really has nothing to do with it.

The 1989 tour invites the obvious question—one that has been asked for the last 20 years: Is this the Stones last tour? Keith is of the opinion that the Stones could play for another 25 years, much like the great blues musicians. Jagger's vision is not quite as far-reaching. Neither a farewell tour nor the start of the next era, the *Steel Wheels* tour was simply the Stones in 1989. What the future holds remains to be seen.

**Opposite page:** *Raising his arm triumphantly, Mick brings the show to a close. The 33-city, 60-show Steel Wheels Tour of North America grossed in excess of 110 million dollars, the most ever for a rock band. After covering North America, the Stones took Japan by storm before moving on to Europe for another 50 shows.*

*In Atlantic City, the last city on the North American leg of the tour, Keith commented, 'It's been more consistent than the others. The boys kicked ass.'*

*They certainly did. Back in the early days (right), did they ever dream it would turn out like this?*

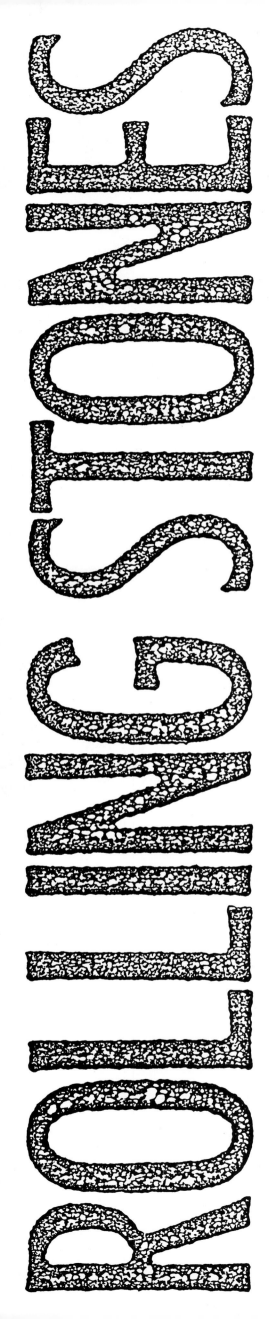

# THE ALBUMS OF THE ROLLING STONES

(dates listed refer to American releases)

*England's Newest Hit Makers,* May 1964

*12 X 5,* October 1964

*The Rolling Stones, Now!,* February 1965

*Out of Our Heads,* July 1965

*December's Children,* November 1965

*Big Hits (High Tide and Green Grass),* March 1966

*Aftermath,* June 1966

*Got Live If You Want It!,* November 1966

*Between the Buttons,* January 1967

*Flowers,* June 1967

*Their Satanic Majesties Request,* November 1967

*Beggar's Banquet,* November 1968

*Through the Past Darkly,* September 1969

*Let It Bleed,* November 1969

*'Get Yer Ya-Ya's Out' The Rolling Stones in Concert,* September 1970

*Sticky Fingers,* June 1971

*Hot Rocks: 1964-1971,* January 1972

*Exile on Main Street,* May 1972

*More Hot Rocks (Big Hits & Fazed Cookies),* December 1972

*Goat's Head Soup,* September 1973

*It's Only Rock 'n' Roll,* October 1974

*Made in the Shade,* June 1975

*Metamorphosis,* June 1975

*Black and Blue,* April 1976

*Love You Live,* September 1977

*Some Girls,* June 1978

*Emotional Rescue,* July 1980

*Sucking in the Seventies,* March 1981

*Tattoo You,* August 1981

*Still Life,* June 1982

*Undercover,* November 1983

*Rewind (1971-1984),* July 1984

*Dirty Work,* March 1986

*Steel Wheels,* August 1989

## THE MOVIES OF THE ROLLING STONES

*The TAMI Show,* 1964

*Charlie is My Darling,* 1965 (unreleased)

*What's on the Flip Side?,* 1966 (unreleased)

*Now Time,* 1967

*A Degree of Murder,* 1967 (score by Brian Jones)

*London in the Sixties,* 1968

*Rock and Roll Circus,* 1968 (unreleased)

*Tonight Let's All Make Love in London,* 1968

*Man to Man,* 1969

*Gimme Shelter,* 1970

*Ned Kelly,* 1970 (Mick Jagger only)

*Performance,* 1970 (Mick Jagger only)

*Sympathy for the Devil (One Plus One),* 1970

*Invocation of My Demon Brother,* 1971

*Ladies and Gentlemen, the Rolling Stones* (at the Marquee Club), 1971

*Cocksucker Blues,* 1972 (unreleased)

*Ladies and Gentlemen, the Rolling Stones Are Back,* 1973

*Ladies and Gentlemen, the Rolling Stones,* 1974

*The Rolling Stones 1978 Tour Film,* 1978

*Let's Spend the Night Together,* 1983

**Above: *Rockin' and rollin' in Philadelphia with Mick Jagger, as the Stones kicked off their sold-out 1981 tour. The tour defended and perpetuated the myth surrounding the World's Greatest Rock and Roll Band.***

# INDEX